OFFICIATING BASKETBALL

A publication for the National Federation of State High School Associations Officials Education Program

Developed by the
American Sport Education Program

Human Kinetics

Library of Congress Cataloging-in-Publication Data

Officiating basketball / developed by the American Sport Education Program.
    p. cm.
"A publication for the National Federation of State High School Associations Officials Education Program."
Includes index.
ISBN 0-7360-4767-0 (soft cover)
    1. Basketball--Officiating--United States--Handbooks, manuals, etc. 2. Basketball--United States--Rules--Handbooks, manuals, etc. I. American Sport Education Program. II. National Federation of State High School Associations. Officials Education Program
GV885.2.O44 2005
796.323'02'022--dc22

ISBN: 0-7360-4767-0

The Web addresses cited in this text were current as of November 2004, unless otherwise noted.

NFHS Officials Education Program Coordinator and Project Consultant: Mary Struckhoff; **Project Writer:** Thomas Hanlon; **Acquisitions Editors:** Renee Thomas Pyrtel and Greg George; **Developmental Editor:** Laura Floch; **Assistant Editor:** Mandy Maiden; **Copyeditor:** Alisha Jeddeloh; **Proofreader:** Coree Clark; **Indexers:** Robert and Cynthia Swanson; **Graphic Designer:** Andrew Tietz; **Graphic Artist:** Tara Welsch; **Photo Manager:** Dan Wendt; **Cover Designer:** Jack W. Davis; **Photographer (cover):** Dan Wendt; **Photographer (interior):** Dan Wendt; photos on pages 1, 8, 13, 27, 119, 124, 126, 132, 135, 140, and 142 © Human Kinetics; **Art Manager:** Kareema McLendon; **Illustrator(s):** Argosy and Mic Greenberg; **Printer:** United Graphics

We thank Normal West High School in Normal, Illinois for assistance in providing the location for the photo shoot for this book.

Copies of this book are available at special discounts for bulk purchase for sales promotions, premiums, fund-raising, or educational use. Special editions or book excerpts can also be created to specifications. For details, contact the Special Sales Manager at Human Kinetics.

Printed in the United States of America   10   9   8   7   6   5   4   3   2   1

Human Kinetics
Web site: www.HumanKinetics.com

United States: Human Kinetics
P.O. Box 5076
Champaign, IL 61825-5076
800-747-4457
e-mail: humank@hkusa.com

Canada: Human Kinetics
475 Devonshire Road Unit 100
Windsor, ON N8Y 2L5
800-465-7301 (in Canada only)
e-mail: orders@hkcanada.com

Europe: Human Kinetics
107 Bradford Road
Stanningley
Leeds LS28 6AT, United Kingdom
+44 (0) 113 255 5665
e-mail: hk@hkeurope.com

Australia: Human Kinetics
57A Price Avenue
Lower Mitcham, South Australia 5062
08 8277 1555
e-mail: liaw@hkaustralia.com

New Zealand: Human Kinetics
Division of Sports Distributors NZ Ltd.
P.O. Box 300 226 Albany
North Shore City
Auckland
0064 9 448 1207
e-mail: blairc@hknewz.com

CONTENTS

PREFACE

In the past 20 years, basketball has evolved into a faster, more athletic game. Players are training and playing year-round and the result is quicker, stronger athletes and a more physical game. Basketball is one of the most difficult sports to officiate because of its speed and physical aspects. *Officiating Basketball* is a key resource for officiating basketball games at the high school level. The mechanics you'll find in this book have been developed by the National Federation of State High School Associations (NFHS) and are used throughout the United States.

You probably know at least a little about basketball but maybe not much about officiating it, or maybe you know lots about both. The objective of *Officiating Basketball* is to prepare you to officiate games regardless of your experience. Specifically, this book will

- introduce you to the culture of officiating basketball,
- tell you what is expected of you as a basketball official,
- explain and illustrate the mechanics of officiating basketball,
- connect the rules of basketball with the mechanics of officiating it and
- serve as a reference for you throughout your officiating career.

Officiating Basketball covers basketball officiating basics, mechanics and specific situations. In part I, you'll read about who basketball officials are and what qualities are found in a good basketball official. Part I also differentiates between high school officiating and officiating at the youth and college levels, and it describes game responsibilities, including pregame and postgame duties. Part II, the meat of the book, describes officials' mechanics for two-person and three-person crews. Part III highlights some key cases from the *NFHS Basketball Case Book,* showing how to apply the rules in action.

Officiating Basketball is a practical how-to guide that's approved by the NFHS. This book is also the text for the *NFHS Officiating Basketball Methods* online course, which has been developed by the American Sport Education Program (ASEP) and the NFHS. To find out how you can register for the online course, visit www.ASEP.com.

NFHS OFFICIALS CODE OF ETHICS

Officials at an interscholastic athletic event are participants in the educational development of high school students. As such, they must exercise a high level of self-discipline, independence and responsibility. The purpose of this code is to establish guidelines for ethical standards of conduct for all interscholastic officials.

- Officials shall master both the rules of the game and the mechanics necessary to enforce the rules, and shall exercise authority in an impartial, firm and controlled manner.
- Officials shall work with each other and their state associations in a constructive and cooperative manner.
- Officials shall uphold the honor and dignity of the profession in all interaction with student-athletes, coaches, athletic directors, school administrators, colleagues and the public.
- Officials shall prepare themselves both physically and mentally, shall dress neatly and appropriately and shall comport themselves in a manner consistent with the high standards of the profession.
- Officials shall be punctual and professional in the fulfillment of all contractual obligations.
- Officials shall remain mindful that their conduct influences the respect that student-athletes, coaches and the public hold for the profession.
- Officials shall, while enforcing the rules of play, remain aware of the inherent risk of injury that competition poses to student-athletes. When appropriate, they shall inform event management of conditions or situations that appear unreasonably hazardous.
- Officials shall take reasonable steps to educate themselves about recognizing emergency conditions that might arise during the competition.

KEY TO DIAGRAMS

 Official

Player with ball

O Offensive players

X Defensive players

→ Officials' path of movement

- - - →

∿∿∿→ Players' path of movement

⟹ Direction of play

PART I

BASKETBALL OFFICIATING BASICS

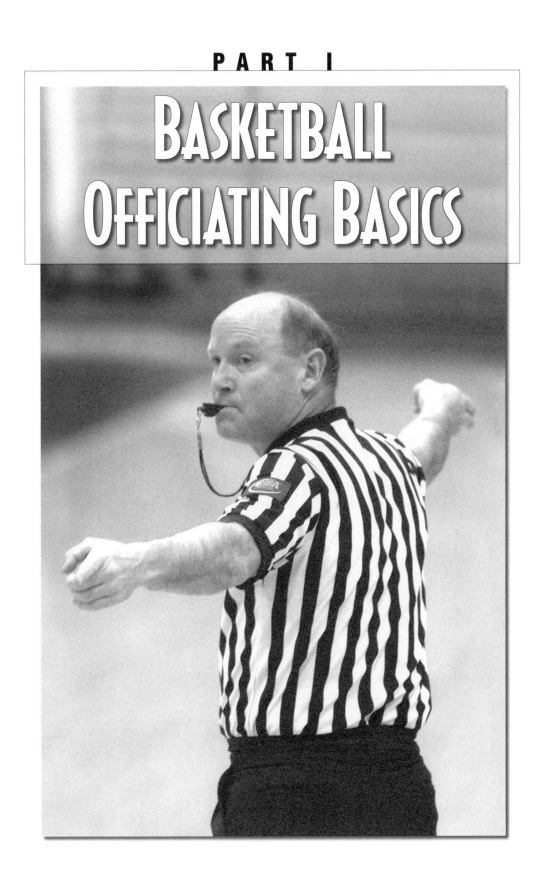

CHAPTER 1

Introduction to Basketball Officiating

Basketball is the nation's most popular high school sport—nearly 1 million students compete on school teams. There are about 16,600 boys' varsity teams and about the same number of girls' varsity teams. Many high schools also have junior varsity teams as well as teams for sophomores and freshmen. This, of course, means that finding and retaining quality officials are a priority for schools. If each school played two varsity games in a given week, the number of officials required to work these games would total nearly 66,000. Include nonvarsity games, and the number of required officials more than doubles.

A good basketball official is a gem. Solid officiating allows two teams to compete without either team having an unfair advantage. As an official, you need a thorough understanding of the rules of the game and the ability to apply those rules correctly. Through this understanding and ability you help provide a safe and fair environment in which athletes may compete. Safety and fairness, after all, are two of your main purposes as a basketball official.

Purpose and Philosophy

You have three main purposes as an official:

1. To ensure fair play by knowing and upholding the rules of the game
2. To minimize risks for the players to the extent that you can
3. To exercise authority in an impartial, firm and controlled manner, as stated in the NFHS Officials Code of Ethics (see page vii)

Let's take a moment to consider all three purposes.

Fair Play

Fair play is at the foundation of all games. Nothing makes players, coaches and fans more irate than the perception that the rules are not being applied correctly and fairly. Competitors want and deserve an equal playing field.

One of the biggest concerns in officiating basketball is making consistent calls, especially when calling offensive charges, defensive blocking and fouls. If you call close fouls on one team, you need to make sure you call them the same way on the other team. To be consistent, officials must be in position to see each play. Although the manual cannot cover every situation, careful study and practice of floor mechanics will allow you to find the proper angle to see each play.

The point is this: To ensure fair play, you have to know the rules and you have to enforce them the same way every time. When you do this, you are on your way to being a good official.

Risk Minimization

Like all sports, basketball has inherent risks of injury. The game is fast and physical. Players dive for loose balls, often colliding. They run full speed on fast breaks and leap high in the air as they go for the layup, exposing themselves to hard landings if they are fouled. The battle for rebounds is fierce, and players can become victims of inadvertent elbows. The chance for injury is part of the game. Still, as an official you need to minimize those risks and respond appropriately when a player is injured. You can do this in four ways:

1. Know and enforce the rules. Many rules were created to minimize the risk of injury.
2. Inspect the court beforehand and report any hazardous conditions to event management.
3. Maintain authority and control in all aspects, especially during action around the area near the backboards and arguments between opponents.
4. Know how to respond to injuries and emergency situations.

Authority

It's vital that you exercise authority in an impartial, firm and controlled manner. You can know the rules backward and forward, but if you can't exercise your authority, you'll have a difficult time officiating a game.

Everyone involved is looking to you to make the proper calls in a manner that doesn't call extra attention to yourself but shows that you know the rules and know how to apply them fairly. They also need to see that you have control over every situation. If you make calls in an indecisive manner or appear not to know the rules, you are headed for trouble, and it is often difficult to regain authority once you lose it.

Fundamental Basketball Rules

Without replicating the *NFHS Basketball Rules Book*—or replacing the need for thoroughly studying it—here are the 20 most important rules in basketball:

1. While the ball is live, a loose ball always remains in control of the team whose player last had control, except in the case of a try or tap for goal.
2. No team or any player is ever in control during a dead ball, jump ball or throw-in, or when the ball is in flight during a try or tap for goal.
3. A goal is made when a live ball enters the basket from above and remains in or passes through, unless it is canceled by a throw-in violation or a player-control foul.
4. The jump ball, throw-in and free throw are the only methods of getting a dead ball live.
5. Neither the dribble nor traveling rule is applicable during the jump ball, throw-in or free throw.
6. It is not possible for a player to travel while dribbling.
7. The only infractions for which points are awarded are goaltending by the defense or basket interference at the opponent's basket.
8. There are three types of violations, each with its own penalty.
9. A ball in flight has the same relationship to the frontcourt or backcourt, inbounds or out of bounds as when it last touched a person or the floor.
10. Personal fouls always involve illegal contact and occur during a live ball, except for common fouls by airborne shooters.
11. The penalty for a single flagrant personal or flagrant technical foul is two free throws and disqualification plus the awarding of the ball to the opponents for a throw-in.
12. Penalties for fouls are administered in the order in which the fouls occurred.
13. A live-ball foul by the offense (the team in control of the ball or last in control if it is loose) immediately kills the ball, unless the ball is in flight during a try or tap for goal. This holds true for the expiration of a quarter or extra period as well. The ball also becomes dead when a player-control foul occurs.

14. The first or only free-throw violation by the offense immediately kills the ball.

15. A double personal foul involves only personal fouls and only two opponents. No free throws are awarded and the ball is put in play by the team entitled to the throw-in under the procedure for alternating possession. A double technical foul involves only technical fouls and only two opponents. No free throws are awarded and the ball is put in play by the team entitled to the throw-in (based on alternating possession) at the division line opposite the table.

16. The official's whistle seldom causes the ball to become dead; it is already dead.

17. Continuous motion applies to tries and taps for field goals and free throws, but it has no significance unless the defense fouls during the time between the beginning of the habitual trying or tapping movement and the moment the ball is clearly in flight.

18. Whether the clock is running or stopped has no influence on whether a goal counts.

19. A ball that touches the front face or edges of the backboard is treated the same as a ball touching the floor inbounds, except that when the ball touches the thrower's backboard it does not constitute part of a dribble.

20. If the ball goes through the basket before or after a player-control foul, the goal does not count.

To gain and maintain authority, you must be decisive and consistent in your calls, retain control at all times and make correct and impartial calls. When you do this you not only maintain your authority, but you uphold the honor and dignity of the profession as well. Coaches and players prefer to have games called by officials who maintain consistent authority, because they know what to expect from such officials. This doesn't mean you never make a mistake; it means you never lose control of the game. Part of maintaining control comes from knowing the rules.

Who Are Basketball Officials?

Officiating basketball is challenging and rewarding. Officiating is a diverse profession, attracting men and women from all walks of life—bankers, insurance agents, business executives, factory workers, postal workers and on and on. Some have played high school, college or amateur ball; others' careers ended with youth basketball. Some are just out of high school; others are retired.

Despite these differences, good officials have much in common. They are critical thinkers who can make decisions in the heat of the moment while maintaining poise. They are peacekeepers and negotiators. They know when and how to stroke an ego without demeaning themselves or harming the integrity of the game. They know when and how to sell a call. They have thick skins and a great deal of patience. They are men and women who love basketball and who strive to achieve appropriate goals. And they are community-oriented people who choose the officiating profession to stay close to the game and give back to a sport that has given much to them.

Principles of Basketball Officiating

Officials are individuals, but they share common goals and principles. As an official, follow these cardinal principles:

- Understand the rules and mechanics. Know the authorized signals and make them promptly and decisively.
- Be on time, be prepared mentally and physically, and keep your uniform in good condition. Don't wear jewelry during the game.
- Maintain good posture on the floor and administer your duties in a businesslike manner.
- Be professional with everyone you come into contact with as an official, including other officials. Be alert, pleasant and firm. Stay calm at all times.
- Don't fraternize with coaches or fans before or during the game.
- Don't use tobacco or alcohol in the vicinity of the court.
- Don't make a report that could be used as a scouting report by a future opponent.

What Makes a Good Official?

To be a good official, you need a combination of qualities, some of which you probably already have. Others you'll develop over time as you gain experience. The same personality traits that make a successful supervisor or director make a successful official. Attention to detail, alertness, and quick but sound reactions are qualities that you must cultivate. Characteristics that distinguish exceptional officiating from average officiating include confidence, decisiveness, courage, mental toughness, good instincts and resolve.

Officials must exhibit authority and maintain order throughout the game.

Expectations for officials are high. Your role on the court is similar to that of a school principal or a police officer. You are expected to be the authority at all times, restoring order to some of the most tenuous circumstances. Fans, coaches and players may not always hold you in the highest regard, but they still count on you for fairness and professionalism at all times.

Like athletes, officials are expected to improve their skills. And like players, officials need a range of skills to excel. Sometimes those skills can almost seem contradictory. For example, to be a good official you have to maintain control of the game yet ensure that the game remains in the players' hands. While the emotions around you fly high, you must remain calm and collected at all times.

You will make mistakes. No one is perfect. Don't be too hard on yourself; simply learn from your mistakes and do your best not to repeat them. Becoming a good official is not easy. It takes commitment, dedication and preparation. You can join the ranks of good officials by following the 12 prerequisites for good officiating:

1. Know the rules.

Rules competence comes from study, preparation and experience. The rules are one of your most useful tools (for others, see "Basketball Official's Tools"). Because you make some decisions more often than others, you'll find that those calls will soon come naturally. Through continual study of different situations, you'll be prepared to make any call.

It's one thing to know the rules and quite another to apply them during a game. As you study the rules, visualize plays. These images will allow you to recognize situations when they occur during games, helping you confidently make the correct calls. Remember, if you don't make your calls confidently, fans, players and coaches will assume that you don't know the rules and they will lose respect for you.

2. Master the lingo.

As you study the rules and gain experience, you'll learn the lingo: bonus free throw, common foul, double foul, team in control, continuous motion and so on. You have to be able to speak the language to communicate with other officials, coaches and players.

3. Master the mechanics.

Your knowledge of the rules might be extensive and your command of the language impressive, but if your mechanics are poor you will have a hard time getting your calls accepted. When a crew of officials uses proper mechanics, no play can occur without one of them being in position to see the play clearly.

Mastery of the mechanics is critical to your success. First, you must learn the most advantageous positions for various situations, and then you must practice coverage so that positioning becomes second nature. You should take the best position possible without getting in the way of any player or the play itself. After games, you should review tapes to look for opportunities to discuss mechanics with your crew or other officials at clinics.

4. Make accurate and decisive calls.

Your first move should be to come to a complete stop, position yourself on the court so that you can see the action and then make your call. Avoid making a call while you're in motion. You need to know where the ball is and if relevant, where the players involved in the play are. After you've assessed the situation, make a decisive call.

Make decisive calls using good timing, but don't rush to judgment. This can be confusing for new officials. They think that in order to be decisive they have to blow their whistle fast. Making decisive calls does not mean rushing to judgment. Watch the whole play from beginning to end, decide if there is a foul or violation, and then blow your whistle.

Indecision conveys a lack of confidence. The more calls you experience, the more assured you become in making the tough calls. Also, making your calls assertively helps get your call accepted. When reporting your calls, speak with authority and certainty. One of your greatest assets is your voice. While avoiding "blasting" those around you, be sure to communicate all calls loudly and clearly so that players, coaches and fans from both teams can understand you.

Sometimes you will not make the right call. When you make a mistake, simply continue to work to the best of your ability. Avoid losing your concentration because of an incorrect call. Don't be overly sensitive to criticism, and never attempt to make up for a call after an error. Each call must stand on its own.

Above all, make all calls when they occur, without thinking about the score and game situation, how it might affect future relations with a coach or school, or what the fans, coaches and players will think. Making calls often takes courage. When you determine before each game that you are going to make every call as it occurs, you take the pressure off yourself. Know that you won't please everyone with your calls and simply focus on making the proper and necessary call.

5. Focus on the court, not the stands.

Be prepared for heckling. Every crowd includes fans that live to insult and distract the officials. You must ignore them. Reacting to fans will never serve you well and will only detract from your ability to call the game. If fans sense that they can get to you, their heckling will only increase. Tune out fans and stay focused on the action.

Your job is to make the right call at the right time. Even if fans, players or coaches become irate, you should maintain a calm demeanor, staying away from anger and frustration. You are counted on to keep the game's temperature under control. Enlist the help of your crewmates in potentially volatile situations, and be prepared to handle such situations.

6. Remain in the background.

The game is about the players, not the officials. Don't draw attention to yourself; execute your duties without fanfare. When you handle your responsibilities with professionalism and confidence, you encourage players, coaches and spectators to accept your decisions. Being overly dramatic gets you noticed, but it also often causes players to lose confidence in you because they perceive you as "showboating." The show must go on, and the players, not you, are the show. You are there to help the show go on fairly and safely.

7. Be professional.

It's okay to be friendly toward players and coaches, but avoid visiting excessively with them immediately before, during or after a game. Never coach a player by giving tips.

Tempers will flare during a game. Remain sensitive to these potentially disruptive conditions. Don't argue with players, coaches or team representatives. Never get emotionally involved. Keep your discussions with such personnel brief. Be courteous, tactful and polite, but don't back down. A professional attitude will often diffuse a problem.

Basketball Official's Tools

Use the following tools to help you learn and grow as an official:

- *The current* NFHS Basketball Rules Book. Get it and learn it backward and forward.
- *Officiating resources.* To hone your skills, use this book and the *Officiating Basketball Mechanics CD (NFHS Edition)*, another product of the NFHS Officials Education Program, which shows animated mechanics, as well as magazines and other resources.
- *Firsthand experience.* Use every officiating experience to improve your ability to officiate and expand your knowledge of the game.
- *Secondhand experience.* Learn from watching good officials, either in person or on tape. Check out their mechanics, how they comport themselves, how they exercise authority, how they deal with coaches and players, and how they make their calls. Consider adapting their procedures to your own style.
- *Crewmates.* Learn from their experience and style, and don't be afraid to discuss plays and other issues before and after games.
- *Clinics and workshops.* Attend as many officiating application seminars as possible. If none are offered in your area, contact veteran officials and recommend that they design one of their own. Call your local schools or recreational organizations about developing workshops.
- *Journal.* Keep a journal as a self-assessment tool, charting areas for improvement, successes, progress and things learned from each game.
- *Self-review.* Secure someone to tape your games so that you can track your progress over the season. Videotapes are excellent learning tools.
- *Review from others.* Invite feedback by requesting fellow officials to watch you and comment on your work.
- *Pre- and postgame meetings.* Pre- and postgame meetings are key learning times for officials, especially beginners. Don't be afraid to admit you don't know something or you need help.

8. Keep control.

You keep control through your knowledge and consistent enforcement of the rules. You also keep control by staying alert for potential trouble. Being in position to observe any questionable contact and having the respect of the players go a long way toward preventing problems. When a player baits an opponent, deal with it immediately. At times, you can call the matter to the attention of the team captain, who can often intervene and stop the baiting without penalty. Otherwise, the only way you can stop the problem is to penalize the player who is doing the baiting.

The point is to be alert for potential problems and use preventive officiating when possible. When that's not possible, maintain control by immediately making the right call.

9. Hustle, hustle, hustle.

To be successful, you have to hustle and be alert at all times. There's no time to rest while the game's in progress. Move briskly, and when appropriate, encourage your fellow officials to do the same. Your posture and appearance communicate your ability to make calls. Always use open body language; avoid folding your arms, putting your hands on your hips, leaning on the scorer's table or frowning.

10. Be a good teammate.

Like the players on the court, you are part of a team—the officiating crew. Support your fellow officials through your actions, words and body language. Be willing to accept responsibility and don't attempt to shift blame to another member of the crew when things go wrong. Never discuss any game decisions with the media and never publicly criticize a fellow official. Respect your fellow officials.

Make a conscientious effort not to infringe on the responsibilities of fellow officials. It is imperative to to talk about court positions and responsibilities before the game so that everyone is clear on their duties. You can avoid embarrassment simply by communicating during the game and sticking together to make sure the right call is made.

11. Stay in shape.

Being in physical shape is important for performing on the court. Today's players are more skilled and athletic than they were 20 years ago. To keep up with them, you have to stay in shape. The speed of the game requires that you maintain stamina so that you can be on the spot to make the proper call. If you aren't physically fit, you're a detriment to the officiating team and the game. Make the commitment to be in shape before the season begins and to maintain your conditioning throughout the season.

12. Be passionate about officiating.

Without passion for the game and for officiating, it's difficult to become a great basketball official. When you bring energy and enthusiasm to your officiating, you're more likely to succeed. The more you give, the more you get back in return.

Officiating at the High School Level

Officiating basketball at the high school level is certainly similar to officiating at lower and higher levels, but there are some aspects that make the high school experience unique.

At youth levels, officials sometimes coach the players, giving them technique tips or allowing them to bend the rules as they learn the game. This does not happen at the high school level, where you simply call the game fairly and authoritatively.

Another difference may be in the number of officials. Many times at youth levels there is only one official. At the college level you could have three-person crews. At the high school level you usually operate in two-official or three-official crews. In chapters 4 and 5 you'll learn the mechanics of these types of crews.

There are rules differences as well. The three-point arc varies; a shot clock is used at the professional level, in college and in some states for high school; the length of the game and size of the court differ; and the free-throw rules differ. Refer to the *NFHS Basketball Rules Book* for other differences.

Regardless of the differences, there are many similarities for officials at the high school level and above in terms of the business of officiating.

At the high school level, an official must call the games fairly and authoritatively.

The Business of Officiating

The key is to treat the game with respect. Officiating might be something you do on the side, but it is also a serious business endeavor.

What does this mean? For one thing, your word is your bond. If you accept a game, be there, and be on time. If you must cancel, call the contest manager as soon as possible. If road conditions or other extenuating circumstances make postponement or cancellation a possibility, talk about this with the contest manager as soon as possible. Be prepared for challenges and handle them appropriately. Check with your state office about officiating high school games. Some states require that you join a local association where games are assigned. In other states you must directly contact the coach or athletic director of each school.

A few don'ts: Don't lobby or beg for a game; don't trade games with officials, coaches or athletic directors; and don't undercut other officials by offering to take games at lower fees. But do market your professional services through the appropriate channels. For example, if you are a new official, you might design a postcard listing your name, qualifications, experience and availability and send it to associations, community and youth organizations as well as relevant sport groups.

As with many business ventures, officiating includes matters such as compensation, insurance and legal concerns.

Compensation and Insurance

Most people don't expect to get rich through officiating, but that doesn't mean you shouldn't discuss compensation when a job opportunity arises. If high school state associations do not establish game fees for officials, officiating fees are generally agreed upon through friendly negotiations between officials and school administrators, who arrive jointly at a fair fee for a particular area and level of play or size of school. Attempts to set fees have met with little success and in some cases have created problems for the officials trying to set the fees.

As an independent contractor you are responsible for reporting and paying all appropriate taxes. Ask your tax adviser any questions you have regarding deductions and related issues. Also, any personal insurance needs are your responsibility. If you have any questions about liability coverage, check with the NFHS Officials Association.

Legal Concerns

All game contracts and agreements should be put in writing to avoid any misunderstanding as to terms and dates. You might consider retaining the services of an attorney to make sure all written agreements are legally sound. Many state officials' associations provide sample contract forms, so check with your association.

Using agreements promotes professionalism and organization. It can also assist with essential record keeping come tax season. What might appear to be a straightforward officiating deal should still be committed to paper. Be prompt and professional in making or responding to requests. Here are a few things to remember in setting up games and keeping records:

1. Always confirm the date, time and location of the game in writing. If you need directions to the location, don't hesitate to ask.

2. About a week before the contest, send a note to the contest manager confirming your participation.

3. File all pertinent agreements and documents, including appropriate receipts and vouchers.

Most associations require some form of reporting, so be sure to promptly submit all paperwork. If you are unclear about something related to the report, call the association. If rating reports are used, send them. As an important part of maintaining the sport's integrity, you are required to report any unusual or unsporting behavior. Do so, and be ready to provide testimony if called upon.

Growing As an Official

Most of this chapter so far has been devoted to what it takes to officiate at the high school level. This section considers some ways you can continue to develop as an official. Getting your foot in the door and beginning to officiate high school games is one matter; continuing to improve as an official is another. It's the officials who experience this growth who are sought out for the big games and who earn the reputation of being a top-notch official.

Here are several ways to continue your development:

- *Stay up on the rules.* Make sure you stay up on changes in the rules. Begin reviewing the rules, including any changes, at least a few months before the season tips off. This studying should continue throughout the season, right up to the last game. Even veteran officials should brush up on the rules before the beginning of the season.

- *Attend workshops and clinics.* Attend rules interpretation meetings and officials' clinics sponsored by your state association or local officials groups. You can also benefit from informal gatherings of officials in your area. If rulings for controversial situations come up in clinics and they don't appear to be covered in the rules book, contact your state association office. They will either know the proper interpretation or they will secure it promptly.

- *Gain experience.* In the early stages of your career, don't hesitate to accept city league, charity, intramural or recreation league games. These contests are excellent opportunities to hone your officiating skills and network with other officials and people in the community. Basketball camps and clinics present another opportunity for practice. There are numerous girls' and boys' instructional camps during the summer; don't miss out on this valuable experience. Coaches and camp administrators are always looking for officials for scrimmages and games.

- *Find a mentor.* Hook up with an outstanding veteran official who is willing to mentor you. Many experienced officials are eager to help and support inexperienced officials. Veteran officials know that the quality of games increases when all officials are competent. There's no such thing as too many top guns.

Talk to your mentor about the challenges you face as an official, and invite reviews of your performances. Discuss ways you can grow, what has worked for the mentor official in terms of personal growth and what pitfalls you need to avoid.

Once you are established in the profession, consider becoming a mentor yourself. By partnering with community organizations and school associations, you can even organize officials' training clinics and camps to encourage interest in the profession.

- *Develop a support network.* Maintaining contact with other officials is another way to stay in the loop. Some officials find it useful to organize small group discussions or meet informally on a regular basis. It may even be possible to have these sessions online. Another idea is to have monthly teleconferences or online conferences. You can research the Internet to find out more about setting up online meetings. Be sure you have a moderator and everyone understands the protocol of the meeting. Or, do it the old-fashioned way: face to face. There's much to be gained from meeting in person if you and other local officials can do so.

- *Connect with national and state associations.* As a high school official, you have the opportunity to become a member of the nation's largest officiating group, the NFHS Officials Association. The NFHS Officials Association offers insurance coverage, education, equipment, newsletters and ongoing support. You also will become a member of your state officials' association, through which clinics and workshops are offered and you can keep up on rules changes and other matters.

Uniforms and Equipment

Your uniform and equipment as an official include the following:

- *Shirt.* You wear a standard black-and-white, pocketless striped shirt with short sleeves and a V-neck. Undershirts should not be visible. You must wear your shirt tucked inside your trousers. The entire crew must wear the same design and style. Wear your state association patch or emblem as specified.
- *Trousers.* These must be black, with no flares.
- *Belt.* If you wear a belt, it should be black.
- *Jacket.* A jacket is recommended for wear before the game. The crew should have the same type and color of jacket (either navy blue or black).
- *Shoes.* These should be entirely black and have black laces.
- *Socks.* Socks should be black.
- *Glasses.* Avoid glasses if possible. If you wear glasses, position them securely. If you wear contact lenses, check their positioning.
- *Whistle.* It is best that your whistle be made of black plastic. If it's metal, it should have a rubber cap.

When you make a serious commitment to officiating, you can continue to learn, improve and advance. If you don't make this commitment, you won't be helping yourself or the sport.

Remember, good officiating is the key to a quality game, one that puts the focus on the players. Never minimize the role that you play in keeping the game on track and under control. Your hard work, preparation and knowledge will go a long way toward keeping the game fun, competitive and fair.

This chapter focused on the foundation of being a basketball official: purpose and philosophy, who are officials and what makes them good, officiating at the high school level, the business of officiating, and continuing to develop as an official. In the next chapter you'll explore game responsibilities and the procedures for carrying out those responsibilities.

CHAPTER 2

GAME PROCEDURES AND RESPONSIBILITIES

L ike players on a basketball team, individual officials are a part of a larger unit. The better the unit works together, the better the game goes. To work well with your crewmates, you need to understand the game procedures and responsibilities that you and other officials must carry out.

In this chapter we'll look at those procedures and responsibilities. First we'll examine the roles of the various officials involved in a game, and then we'll move on to pregame, game and postgame responsibilities.

Officials' Roles

Several officials play a role in basketball games, including a referee, one or two umpires, an alternate official, a timer and a scorer. Here we describe each of these roles and how the officials work together. The roles of referees and umpires are further defined throughout the chapter.

The referee is the head official, meaning he or she is in charge of the game. The referee tosses the ball up for the center jump to begin the game and each overtime period. Duties range from inspecting all equipment before the start of the game to approving the final score. The referee decides disagreements among officials and makes decisions on any issues not specifically covered in the rules. There is only one referee on the court.

Along with the referee, the umpires are responsible for carrying out the procedures of the game. The duties of the umpires and referee are dictated by their position and coverage on the court; their mechanics are the focus of chapters 4 and 5.

Sometimes an alternate official is on hand in uniform and jacket, prepared to step in and officiate in case a scheduled official is unable to begin or complete a game. The alternate official sits at the scorer's table and aids the scorer and timer, keeping a written record of fouls called, the number of the player committing the foul, the number of the shooter, the number of free throws and the time that the foul occurred. This official's record helps the game officials sort out scoring and timing errors and any other correctible errors.

The timer starts and stops the clock according to the officials' signals. The timer notes when each half is about to start and warns the referee so teams can be notified at least three minutes before each half. The timer also has a stopwatch for clocking time-outs and sounds a warning signal 15 seconds before an intermission or time-out expires and 20 seconds before a 30-second time-out expires. The complete duties of the timer are listed in the *NFHS Basketball Rules Book;* read them and become familiar with them.

The scorer records the names and numbers of the players, records field goals made and free throws made and missed, keeps a running summary of points scored, records fouls and notifies officials when a player is disqualified on fouls and when a bonus free-throw situation occurs, and keeps track of each team's time-outs. For the scorer's complete duties, see the *NFHS Basketball Rules Book.*

Pregame Procedures and Responsibilities

Your duties as an official begin well before tip-off. You should arrive at the game site at least an hour before the game and report to the athletic administrator. The athletic administrator will direct you to the dressing room, where you and the other officials can change into your uniforms and hold a pregame meeting. The referee conducts the meeting, but it should consist of open communication between all officials, including the timer and scorer if possible. Here are some of the items you should cover:

- Decide who will be the referee, unless this has already been determined.
- Check the correct time and the starting time of the game.
- Check whistles, and make sure everyone carries a spare.
- Confirm the use of authorized signals only and go through the signals if necessary.
- Discuss any special ground rules for the gym, unusual plays, new rules and so on.
- Review injury situations, including rules for bleeding players and determining when a player is unconscious.

- Reinforce the emphasis on sporting behavior and discuss how to handle unsporting behavior.
- Discuss areas of coverage for the lead official and trail official, and center official if operating in a three-person crew.

The officiating crew should enter the court together at least 15 minutes before game time. The timer and scorer take their seat at the scorer's table. If there are two officials—a referee (R) and an umpire (U) on the court, they should stand on the side of the court opposite the table, about 28 feet from the nearest end line (see figure 2.1). From these vantage points, the officials can supervise the pregame warm-up.

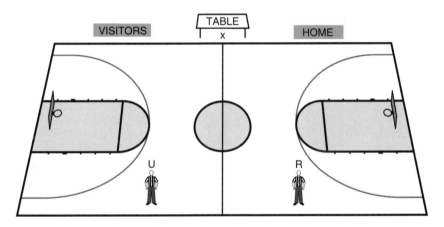

FIGURE 2.1　Officials' positions for pregame warm-up in a two-person crew.

If there are three officials (two umpires and a referee), they should stand as shown in figure 2.2.

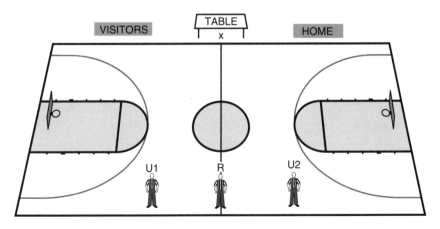

FIGURE 2.2　Officials' positions for pregame warm-up in a three-person crew.

See the following pregame checklists to become familiar with the duties of the referee and umpire before the game. Begin your duties as soon as you enter the court and complete them quickly, but make sure you're thorough. If you're inexperienced, you might want to carry a reference card with the pregame checklist on it until the process becomes natural.

Pregame Checklists

Referee

This checklist includes a timetable to help you proceed with your pregame duties. As stated, 15 minutes before the game you should be in position on the court. From there, your duties are as follows:

12 minutes before game time

❏ Introduce yourself to the captains at center court. The umpires should assist you in getting the team captains.

❏ Go over any special ground rules and unusual conditions with the captains.

10 minutes before game time

❏ Go to the scorer's table. Designate the official timepiece and timer and the official score book and scorer. If the scorer and timer were not present at the pregame meeting, talk with them to make sure that they understand their responsibilities during the game. If they are not seated together, recommend that they sit next to each other.

❏ Sign the score book.

❏ Review signals for conveying information to and from the scorer's table.

❏ Observe the baskets, boundaries, crowd and extraneous apparatus to see if special ground rules are necessary. Be sure the net is loose enough to let the ball drop through.

❏ Count the number of players on the visiting team and secure similar information from the umpire regarding the home team. Verify this information with the scorer. Verify starters are marked.

❏ Check the game balls. Drop the balls from six feet, and if they don't bounce 49 to 54 inches, notify the athletic administrator.

❏ Check the game clock and other timing equipment.

❏ Check the device used to indicate substitutions and the end of a period.

❏ If you're working in a two-person crew, you will observe the visiting team. If you're working in a three-person crew, the umpires will observe both teams while you attend to your designated pregame duties.

3 minutes before game time

❑ If players are not on the court, notify each team that there are three minutes to go before game time. Do this before the start of the second half as well.

1 1/2 minutes before game time

❑ Go to the scorer's table and greet the head coaches. Address your expectations for sporting behavior and verify with head coaches that team members are legally and properly equipped.

❑ Stand at attention for the national anthem.

❑ Remove your coat during the introduction of the players. Often the officials take their jackets back to the locker room when the teams leave the floor. If teams do not return to the dressing room, at least one official should remain on the court.

❑ Go to center court to begin the game.

If the teams return to the dressing room before the game, go to the scorer's table and wait there, or, if you prefer, go to the dressing room with your crewmates and return to the court when the teams return.

Umpire

In a crew of three officials, umpire 1 (U1) is responsible for fulfilling the following duties with the home team and umpire 2 (U2) is responsible for fulfilling the same duties with the visiting team. If you are the only umpire, you are responsible for checking the home team while the referee checks the visiting team. Begin this checklist as soon as you get on the court.

❑ Check uniforms, numbers and other apparel for legality, including undershirts and undergarments.

❑ Report to the referee if any player is wearing jewelry; elbow, hand, finger, wrist or arm guards; or a cast or brace made of hard and unyielding leather, plaster, metal or any other hard substance, even if it's covered with padding.

❑ Report to the referee any player wearing illegal headwear. Secure authorization from the coach if the state association has approved the headwear.

❑ Determine whether ball runners are available to retrieve the ball at each end if the court has wide out-of-bounds areas or is on a raised platform.

❑ Count the number of players on whichever team you are responsible for and report to the referee.

From *Officiating Basketball* by ASEP, 2005, Champaign, IL: Human Kinetics.

Game Procedures and Responsibilities

Here we provide an overview of the responsibilities of the referee and the umpire during a game. There's not a great deal of difference between the referee and umpire; as noted earlier, the officials are equally responsible for the conduct of the game. Remember, no official can question decisions made by other officials within the bounds of those officials' duties. However, referees do have some specific duties:

- Tossing the ball in the center circle for all jump balls
- Verifying whether a goal counts if the officials disagree
- Intervening when the timers and scorers disagree and correcting timing errors
- Conferring with scorers and all game personnel on important matters
- Noting the direction of the alternating-possession arrow to start the second, third and fourth quarters
- Declaring a forfeit when conditions warrant

If you are an umpire, you are charged with making all calls within your coverage area (coverage is detailed in chapters 4 and 5) and assisting the referee as required.

Duties for all officials include the following:

- Notifying captains that play is about to begin
- Granting time-outs
- Beckoning substitutes to enter the court
- Putting the ball into play
- Notifying a coach when a player is disqualified
- Determining when the ball is dead
- Administering penalties
- Signaling a three-point goal by raising two arms overhead
- Silently and visibly counting seconds to administer the throw-in, free throw, backcourt and closely guarded rules
- Reporting a team warning for delay to the scorer and then to the coach

Conferences and Unusual Situations

Sometimes a conference with both coaches is warranted, such as in the case of correctable errors. Involve both head coaches in the discussion.

When you need to, ask one of your partners for help to make sure you get the call right. Examples of times when you might need help include out-of-bounds situations, whether a field goal was a two-pointer or a three-pointer, possible tipped-ball situations or an off-the-ball foul.

If a fight occurs, determine which players should be disqualified, including any bench personnel who leave the bench during the fight. You cannot use video or replay to identify offenders. In states where a coaching box is used, inform the coach that he or she lost the privilege of using that box because of an indirect or direct technical foul. The coach must remain on the bench from then on.

Substitutions

If you are the official with the ball, before putting it into play glance at the scorer's table to see if a substitute has reported and is ready to enter. If this is the case, beckon the substitute to enter. Substitutes must enter promptly; failure to do so is a technical foul. Count the number of players on the court before putting the ball into play.

Once a player has been replaced, he or she cannot reenter the game until the next substitution opportunity after the clock has started.

If the scorer's horn or the game horn sounds for a substitution too close to when the ball is to become live, ignore the horn until the next dead ball. If the substitute comes onto the court, send him or her back to the table to wait for the next dead ball. If you erroneously allow a substitute to replace a designated jumper or free thrower, you can't correct the error after the ball becomes live unless the correctable-error rule is involved.

End of First Half

When the first half ends, stand with your crewmates three-quarters of the way between the center circle and the sideline opposite the scorer's table as teams go to their locker rooms. After both benches have cleared, all officials should walk together to the scorer's table.

If you are the referee, your primary duties at the end of the first half include checking and approving the score, confirming which team will have the ball at the beginning of the third quarter and making sure the alternating-possession arrow is pointed in the correct direction, and discussing any concerns or special situations with table personnel. You should also check with the timer to have the teams and officials notified at least three minutes before the second half is to begin. Leave the ball at the scorer's table, then leave the court with your crewmates and go to your dressing room.

Once you are in the dressing room, relax, replenish your fluids and catch your breath. Briefly review the first half with your crewmates and discuss any necessary adjustments. Return to the court when you're notified that there are three minutes remaining in the intermission.

Check floor conditions before the second half begins, and assume the same position you did to observe the pregame warm-up. Shortly before the second half begins, check in with the scorer's table to note any substitutions, inform the coaches who gets the ball, and secure and give the ball to the proper team for the throw-in to begin the third quarter. The referee conducts the throw-in.

Extra Periods

Before each extra period, as the referee, you should review overtime procedures with the timers, scorers and captains. Teams should remain in the bench area during the one-minute intermission. Overtime begins with you tossing the ball for the jump.

Postgame Procedures and Responsibilities

At the end of a game, as referee, your immediate duty is to approve the final score. Once you've approved the score, promptly jog off the floor with your crewmates, returning to your dressing room. Don't seek to avoid or contact the coaches, and don't make any statements to the media.

The officials' jurisdiction ends when all officials have left the visible confines of the playing area. Once inside the dressing room, change into your street clothes while discussing any pertinent issues with your crewmates. Of course, if your crewmates are of the opposite sex, talk to them either before you enter your dressing rooms or after you leave them. Remember to report any irregularities or flagrant situations to the state association office as soon as possible, following the association's reporting guidelines.

These are your essential responsibilities before, during and after a game. Know them, carry them out well and support your crewmates. In the next chapter we'll move from general principles and responsibilities to the nitty-gritty details: the mechanics of officiating.

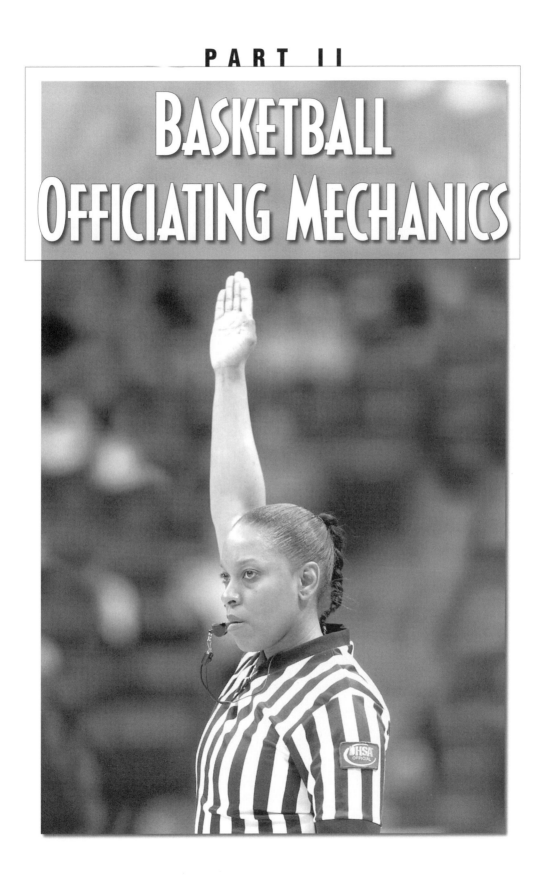

PART II

BASKETBALL
OFFICIATING MECHANICS

CHAPTER 3

ESSENTIAL MECHANICS

Understanding the rules of the game is important to your success as an official, but no less important is your ability to execute the mechanics of officiating, including how you position yourself on the court, what areas you cover, how you work with your crew members and how you communicate calls.

Some mechanics depend on the number of officials, but many remain the same regardless of crew size. In this chapter we'll explore three main areas of general mechanics:

- Basic principles
- Basic procedures and mechanics
- Communicating with crewmates

Basic Principles

Whether there are two or three officials on the court, there is always a lead official and a trail official. In three-person crews, the third person is the center official, whose role is described in chapter 5.

Following are descriptions of the basic duties and movements of the lead and trail officials.

Lead Official

In general, the lead official is ahead of the ball on all plays and the trail official is behind the ball on all plays. Rarely are the officials directly opposite each other as they move up and down the court.

When you are the lead official, you set up on the baseline in frontcourt. You are primarily responsible for play under the basket. As lead official (L), you cover the sideline and the nearest end line while the trail official (T) covers the division line. You are responsible for signaling three-point attempts taken below the free-throw line extended on your side of the court (see figure 3.1). You should remain in the area for which you are responsible and should try to work about four to six feet off the end line.

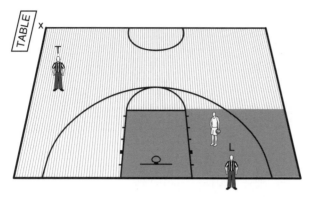

FIGURE 3.1   Lead official's normal responsibilities and area of coverage.

You are responsible for play all the way over to the sideline on your side of the basket, so you must be prepared to move wider when necessary to get an angle on the play (see figure 3.2).

When you are lead official, you may have to adjust your position to provide ball-side assistance when the ball and the majority of players are on the trail official's side of the court (see figure 3.3). However, use this technique sparingly, as it leaves one side of the court completely uncovered. You should consult your state's high school association before using this technique because they might have guidelines for it.

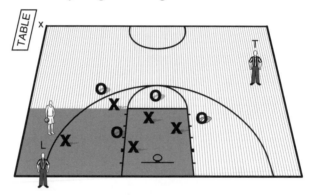

FIGURE 3.2   Lead official in position when play is spread.

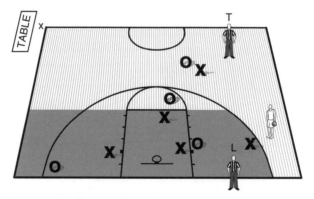

FIGURE 3.3   Lead official providing ball-side assistance when the majority of players are on the trail official's side.

When moving from one end of the floor to the other, you should look over your inside shoulder, never turning your back on the play (see figure 3.4). When a team is using a pressing defense, you should position yourself to assist the trail official (see figure 3.5).

A few more responsibilities are not unique to the lead official or trail official and can fall on the shoulders of either:

FIGURE 3.4 Lead official looking over the inside shoulder while moving downcourt.

- When the player with the ball starts a drive to the basket from any official's area, that official has the player and the ball all the way to the basket. The play happens too quickly for coverage to switch in the middle of the action, so the trail official may be responsible for a drive to the basket even though the lead official is primarily responsible for play under the basket (see figure 3.6).

- Both officials are responsible for administering the five-second count (see figure 3.7, a and b) when a closely guarded player in

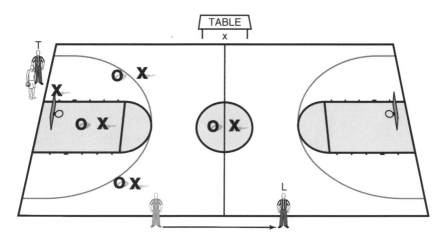

FIGURE 3.5 Lead official in position to assist the trail official when a team uses a pressing defense.

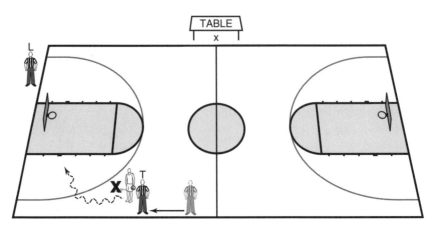

FIGURE 3.6 Trail official's responsibility for a player driving to the basket with the ball when the drive begins in the trail official's area.

FIGURE 3.7 *(a and b)* Official giving a visible count.

the frontcourt holds or dribbles the ball. While any official can give the five-second count, typically the trail official does so because of positioning. The official who begins the five-second count maintains the count until the count end. Switch hands when going directly from one count to another.

- Both officials are responsible for calling three-second lane violations, though the lead official has the primary obligation because of play under the basket.

Trail Official

The trail official is normally behind the ball on all plays. When you are the trail official, you are responsible for covering the backcourt and the outer part of the frontcourt (see figure 3.8). Also, be prepared to work a wide arc as dictated by ball movement (see figure 3.9), observe the flight of the ball on a try, and call backcourt and division-line violations.

As the trail official, on a try or tap you should take at least one step toward the near end line to be in position to observe goaltending, basket interference and rebounding action. You are also responsible for signaling three-point attempts all the way around the top of the key and for signaling successful three-point baskets, goaltending and basket interference.

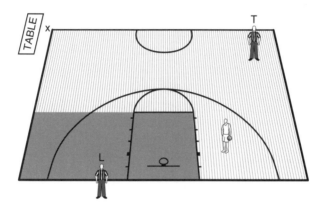

FIGURE 3.8   Trail official's responsibilities and area of coverage.

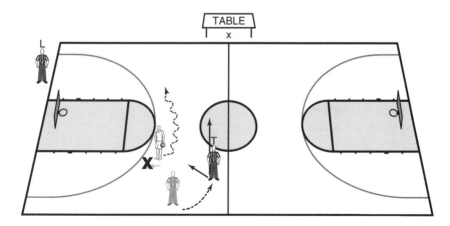

FIGURE 3.9   Trail official working a wide arc as dictated by ball movement.

Basketball Officiating Terminology

You need to know many terms to operate effectively as an official. Here are a few of them:

- *Switch:* A switch happens during the dead ball after one official calls a foul or violation. In a two-person crew, officials always change positions after each foul call. The official not making the foul call (the free official) is responsible for watching the players and making sure the switch takes place once the calling official returns from reporting the foul. Switches for a three-person crew are explained in chapter 5.
- *Closedown:* Closedown is when an official takes a step or two toward the ball or basket based on ball movement or a shot being taken. For example, a trail official will close down toward the end line as the ball moves in that direction, and a lead official will close down toward the nearest lane line as the ball moves toward the basket.
- *Ball side:* The location of the ball in the frontcourt. If you divide the court down the middle from end line to end line using the basket as a center point, ball side is the side of the court where the ball is located.
- *Strong side:* The side the lead official is on.
- *Weak side:* The side opposite the lead official.
- *Table side:* The side of the court where the scorer's table is located.
- *Opposite side:* The side of the court opposite the scorer's table.

Basic Procedures and Mechanics

Positioning is vital to your ability to see and make calls. You need to understand positioning principles for both two-person and three-person crews so you can maintain proper positioning at all times. Positioning depends on the number of officials, ball movement and game flow. When you and your crewmates carry out proper positioning, at least one official will be in position to clearly see a play.

Positioning principles involve understanding each official's primary coverage area. Earlier in this chapter we covered general positioning responsibilities of the lead and trail officials, and in chapter 4 we discuss these responsibilities in greater depth. In chapter 5, we cover positioning for a three-person crew. Study these mechanics until they become second nature and you'll naturally move into position throughout the game without having to think hard about where you should be. This will allow you to focus on the ball and the players.

Along with positioning, your ability to signal is vital to your effectiveness. Signaling is the primary way to indicate what happened on the court to other officials (including the scorer and timer), players, and bench personnel. If you can't signal well, you can't communicate well.

Signal quality is crucial. Make your signals clean, crisp and precise, leaving no doubt as to your call. Your calls might be accurate, but if you use weak, vague signals, people may doubt the call's authenticity. For example, when stopping the clock you must raise a straight arm with the hand closed in a fist to indicate a foul or open to indicate a violation. If your arm is bent or loose, it can convey uncertainty, telling players, coaches and fans that you are unsure of your call.

You should give signals away from your body so that they can be clearly seen. Don't shadow your face with your signals as you speak, because this makes it difficult to see the signals and understand your verbal call.

In the rest of this section we'll explore signaling mechanics that apply to all officials, regardless of whether you're working in a two-person or three-person crew. For a complete set of illustrations, see the appendix of NFHS officiating basketball signals starting on page 145.

Jump Balls

A jump ball begins the game and extra periods. It is conducted in the center circle, with one player jumping for each team.

All officials are responsible for counting the players of both teams before a jump ball. If play begins and one team has six players on the court, it's a technical foul. If a team has four players on the court, it's not a technical foul, but the team cannot bring in a fifth player until the clock has stopped and the player is waved in by an official.

Facing the scorer's table, the referee tosses the ball. If you are the referee, sound your whistle before the toss to alert the players and table officials that play is about to begin. Remove the whistle from your mouth and then toss the ball straight up between the two players who are jumping (see figure 3.10, a-c). Make your toss slightly higher than either player can jump, somewhere around basket height. Practice tossing the ball and find the method that works best for you. If a toss is poor, any official can and should blow the whistle. In that case you should prepare for another jump, with no time run off the clock.

As the referee, you are responsible for the action of the jumpers, however, if there is a violation before a jumper legally touches the ball, the umpire should blow the whistle and signal the time-out because you have removed your whistle from your mouth. If there is no violation before the toss is touched, the clock should start when the ball is legally touched. If the touch is followed by a violation, such as a jumper catching the ball after it has been tapped, stop the clock by sounding the whistle and signaling the timer to stop the clock.

FIGURE 3.10　*(a-c)* Official administering the jump ball.

Once you make a successful toss and play begins, wait until the direction of the play has been established and the umpire has committed to a direction before assuming your position. The trail official should check the table to make sure the directional arrow is set correctly after one team gains control of the jump ball.

Throw-Ins

Throw-ins are used whenever a ball is put in play from out of bounds. Once the throwing player has the ball, it must be released before five seconds elapse or the ball will be turned over to the other team.

If you are the administering official, your responsibilities include the activity of the thrower and the players near the thrower. The other official or officials are responsible for players at a distance. Watch for requests for time-outs and substitutions. If the time-out or substitution request is made when it cannot be honored, ignore the request.

The main concerns of a throw-in are the designated spot (if there is one) and throw-in mechanics.

Designated Spot

Where a throw-in occurs depends on the situation (see figure 3.11). To begin the second, third or fourth quarter, the throw-in takes place at the division line opposite the table as shown in figure 3.12. The referee administers these throw-ins. If you are the referee, you indicate the color and direction, designate the throw-in spot, sound the whistle to alert players that play is about to begin and place the ball at the thrower's disposal. Be sure to make eye contact with your partner before handing the ball to the thrower.

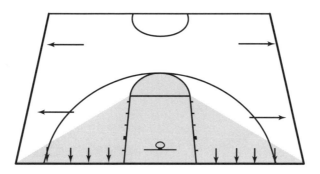

FIGURE 3.11   Throw-in spot designations.

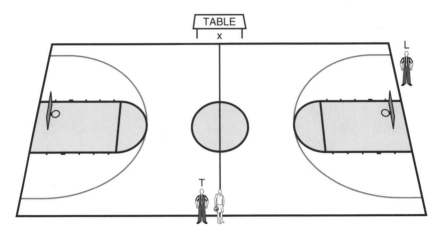

FIGURE 3.12   Location for a throw-in when beginning a quarter.

For alternating possession in other situations, the official responsible for the line designates the throw-in spot and administers the throw-in.

After a technical foul, the throw-in takes place at the division line on the side of the court opposite the table. The throw-in team should make a player available without appreciable delay. If a player is not ready, the ball is placed on the floor and at the disposal of any throw-in team player (see figure 3.13, a-c).

FIGURE 3.13   *(a-c)* Ball at any player's disposal.

Throw-In Mechanics

When you administer a throw-in on an end line, make sure you're not between the player and the basket, and then hand (frontcourt) or bounce (backcourt) the ball to the thrower. When you administer a throw-in on a sideline, bounce the ball to the thrower (see figure 3.14a). Before you hand or bounce the ball to the player, make eye contact with your partners and the table and glance at the clock. Your whistle should be in your mouth, and your arm farthest from the player should be up in preparation for starting the clock (see figure 3.14b). If the throw-in is after a goal, allow the thrower a reasonable amount of time to secure the ball at the end line before beginning the five-second count (see figure 3.14c). Your count should be silent and visible.

Following a charged time-out, intermission or unusual delay, the administrating official sounds the whistle to indicate play is about to begin. If the clock has stopped, signal to start the clock when the released ball touches a player who is inbounds.

In certain situations, if the defending team commits a throw-in plane violation you must first signal the scorer to record a team warning and then report the violation to the team's coach. Give one warning per team and assess a team technical foul for any subsequent plane violations.

a   b   c

FIGURE 3.14 *(a-c)* Official administering a throw-in on a sideline.

Here are a few final notes on throw-ins:

- All throw-ins made from a designated spot at the end line are made from outside the free-throw lane extended (see figure 3.15).

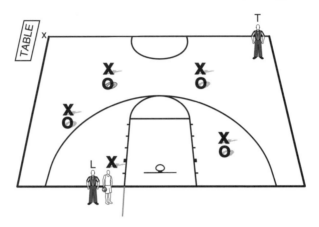

FIGURE 3.15   Throw-in on the end line outside the lane-line extended.

- If the scorer's horn or the game horn sounds, either official may stop the action with a whistle if the ball is not yet live. If the ball is live or the throw-in has started, ignore the horn.
- If two or more teammates take adjacent positions parallel to a boundary line and are within three feet of it, hold up play if an opponent wants to move between them (see figure 3.16).

FIGURE 3.16   Stacking on an inbounds play.

- Use the proper signal (see figure 3.17, a and b) to indicate that running-the-end-line privileges are in effect when the clock has been stopped.

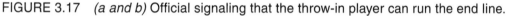

FIGURE 3.17 *(a and b)* Official signaling that the throw-in player can run the end line.

Fouls

Fouls are one of the most common calls. Here are the mechanics for calling and reporting a foul:

1. Sound your whistle with a single, sharp blast while raising one hand, fist clenched, straight above your head (see figure 3.18). This informs the timer to stop the clock and alerts the scorer that a foul has occurred. If you wish to clarify who the foul is on, you may extend your other hand, palm down, toward the fouling player's hips.

2. While holding the foul signal, move near the fouling player, stop and state the shirt color and number.

3. Verbally call out the free-throw shooter's number. Visually signal the number of free throws to the other officials. If the foul is to result in a throw-in, indicate the throw-in spot.

FIGURE 3.18 Official signaling that a foul has occurred.

4. If a goal is scored, signal the scorer to count it. If the ball goes in the basket, it is the responsibility of the free official to communicate that information to the calling official.

5. Lower your foul signal, quickly move to the foul-reporting area (see figure 3.19) and indicate the nature of the foul (see figure 3.20, a-h).

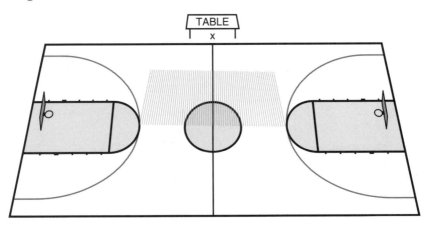

FIGURE 3.19   Foul-reporting area.

Reporting a Foul

When you report a foul or communicate with the scorer's table in general, be sure to do the following:

- Move toward the table and come to a complete stop. Stand erect.
- Make eye contact with the scorer and make your report.
- Speak slowly and clearly and signal numbers with one hand as you speak.
- Indicate the nature of the foul by giving the appropriate NFHS officiating basketball foul signal (see the appendix beginning on page 145).
- If free throws are to be attempted, indicate the number of throws by using one hand, two hands if the bonus is in effect. The scorer will notify the nearest official when the bonus goes into effect.

Be sure your palm faces the scorer when you indicate numbers, and don't jab or spin your hand when signifying double digits. Also, don't verbally repeat numbers. For example, saying, "Foul is on red thirty-four, three four" is confusing. Simply say, "Red thirty-four."

Also avoid moving while signaling, getting too close to the table and not signaling against a clear background. Moving while delivering a report means that the scorer has to work to understand what you are communicating, and there is no need to go all the way over to the scorer's table.

FIGURE 3.20 Official signaling *(a)* block, *(b)* hold, *(c)* hand check, *(d)* push, *(e)* illegal use of hands, *(f)* player-control foul, *(g)* intentional foul and *(h)* double foul.

During a foul situation, observe the activity around each team's bench and penalize infractions when necessary. Be sure to complete your communication with the table before admitting a substitute or acknowledging a time-out request.

If you are the calling official on a double foul or a false double foul, go to the table to see that the fouls are properly charged and that neither player has five fouls. No free throws are awarded for a double personal foul, double technical foul or simultaneous technical foul by both teams; in these cases play resumes with an alternating-possession throw-in. Administer penalties for false double fouls in the order in which the fouls occurred.

If the foul results in a player's disqualification, the noncalling official (two-person crew) or new table-side official (three-person crew) notifies the coach and administers the substitution.

Free Throws

How you administer free throws depends on whether you're in a two-person or three-person crew. However, there are some common procedures. Regardless of crew size, if you are the lead official, you should do the following:

1. Secure the ball until all signals are completed and officials are in position.
2. Check to see that the lane spaces are properly filled.
3. Glance at the table for substitutes.
4. Step into the lane and visually and verbally indicate the number of throws.
5. Bounce the ball to the thrower and then back out of the lane. Take a position about four feet from the nearest lane line, and approximately three feet off the end line (see figure 3.21).

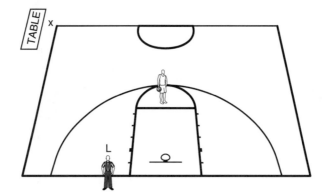

FIGURE 3.21   Proper positioning of lead official after bouncing the ball to the shooter.

6. Watch the first marked lane space on the near lane and all the lane spaces on the opposite side for violations and give the appropriate signal when violations occur (see figure 3.22).

7. If the final throw is to be followed by a throw-in, at the proper time signal to start the clock.

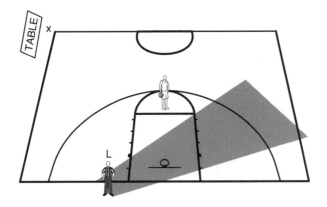

FIGURE 3.22   Lead official's lane-coverage responsibilities during a free throw.

If an opponent makes contact with the free thrower or a huddle delays the administration of a free throw, report a team warning to the scorer and the coach. Each team is allowed one warning for such a delay, after which they are given a team technical foul. Once time has expired for the fourth quarter or any extra period, no free throws should be attempted unless the points could affect the outcome of the game.

Violations

When you observe a violation such as traveling, over-and-back or a three-second violation, you should do the following:

1. Give a single, sharp whistle blast and raise one arm above your head, fingers extended, to stop the clock (see figure 3.23).

FIGURE 3.23   Official signaling to stop the clock after a violation.

2. Move toward the area where the violation occurred, stop and signal the nature of the violation (see figure 3.24, a-e).

3. Point toward the throw-in team's basket and call out their shirt color. Be sure both teams understand who gets the ball.

4. Indicate the throw-in spot.

FIGURE 3.24   Official signaling (a) travel, (b) illegal dribble, (c) over-and-back or palming or carrying the ball, (d) three-second violation and (e) five-second violation.

5. Make sure you do not turn your back on the players when giving signals or indicating direction.

6. Make eye contact with your partners before placing the ball at the disposal of the thrower. After each official is in position, give the thrower the ball, back away and start the throw-in count.

For a free-throw violation by the free thrower or a teammate, follow the same procedure as for a floor violation if no other free throw is to follow. The throw-in spot is normally on the end line at the nearest out-of-bounds spot.

For a free-throw violation by the defensive team, give the delayed violation signal (see figure 3.25), but do not sound the whistle until the free throw has ended. If the free throw is successful, ignore the violation. If the throw is not successful, award a substitute free throw. If this substitute throw is the first throw of a one-and-one bonus penalty and is successful, it will be followed by the extra throw. Following a violation, the clock should not start after an unsuccessful free throw. When in doubt, signal for a time-out when you detect the violation.

When a defensive player commits a free-throw violation and then an offensive player commits a violation in a marked lane space, ignore the second infraction that was made. However, if the second infraction is by the free thrower or a teammate behind the arc, it is a simultaneous violation. If a simultaneous violation occurs on the first of two or three free throws, cancel the throw and award the other free throws. If the simultaneous violation occurs on the last throw, resume play with an alternating-possession throw-in. If disconcertion by a defensive player is followed by a violation by the free thrower, award a substitute free throw.

FIGURE 3.25   Official signaling a delayed violation.

Time-Outs

You need to understand several aspects of time-outs, including

- time-out requests,
- time-out mechanics and
- injury time-outs.

Time-Out Requests

Grant a time-out when a player or head coach orally or visually requests one and when the ball is in player control or is dead. After a successful free throw or field goal, any player or head coach can request a time-out. However, once the thrower has the ball on a throw-in, it is too late for the opponents to request a time-out. After a free thrower has the ball, any team member or that team's head coach can be granted a time-out, but the opponent cannot.

Do not grant a time-out after a foul until the scorer has the necessary information, substitutes have been beckoned or an injured or disqualified player has been replaced. Also, don't grant a time-out during an interrupted dribble.

You should grant a request for an excess time-out, but penalize it with a technical foul. Allow the team the full time and charge the technical foul to them. You can suspend play without charging a team time-out to permit a player to correct or replace eyeglasses or lenses. You should not stop the clock to allow a player to tie their shoelace.

If the scorer's horn sounds while the ball is live or is about to become live, you can choose to ignore it or honor it. Remember, it's the official's whistle that causes the ball to become or remain dead.

Time-Out Mechanics

Here are the mechanics for granting a time-out:

1. Sound your whistle while giving the signal to stop the clock.
2. Let the players clear the floor before turning your back to them to report the time-out.
3. As you move to the reporting area, look for the coach of the team calling the time-out to see what type of time-out to charge (full or 30-second).
4. Within the reporting area, give the appropriate time-out signal, verbally indicate the team color, and verbally and visually state the number of the player requesting the time-out. If the head coach is

making the request, form a "C" with your hand. Then visually and verbally direct the timer to begin the time-out period. Notify the coach when all allotted time-outs have been used.

Positioning during a time-out depends on the size of the crew and is explained more fully in the following chapters on two-person and three-person crews. In general, you should maintain good posture and stay alert during a time-out. For 30-second time-outs, you and your partner should position yourselves at the top of each free-throw circle arc. For 60-second time-outs, you should position yourselves at the nearest block of the free-throw lane, opposite the table. During the intermission between quarters (first and second, third and fourth), your position is the same as for a 60-second time-out.

At the warning signal (the first horn), the officials should step toward the team huddles and notify the coaches and players by raising an index finger and saying, "First horn." Try to make eye contact with the captain or assistant coach. Then move to your proper position to resume play.

Make sure that each team has five players on the court. After the second horn sounds to end the time-out, the administering official sounds the whistle to indicate that play is ready to resume. Signal to start the clock.

Injury Time-Outs

If a player is injured, call an officials' time-out to protect the player, if necessary. When you need to call an injury time-out, do so and beckon the player's bench immediately. The injured player must leave the game until the next opportunity to reenter after the clock has started, unless that player's team calls a time-out. If an apparently injured player is ready to resume play within a few seconds and the bench has not been beckoned, the player may remain in the game. In that case, resume play as quickly as possible.

It's up to the officials to determine if a player has been rendered unconscious. A player who was rendered unconscious must leave the game and cannot return unless a physician provides written authorization. Do not touch an unconscious player.

If a player appears to be bleeding, has an open wound or has an excessive amount of blood on the uniform or body, the player must leave the game and not return until after the clock has started and a substitution opportunity occurs, unless his or her team calls a time-out. All bleeding must be stopped, open wounds covered and blood cleaned off the uniform (the uniform can also be changed) before the player can participate.

Taps or Tries for Goal

When a tap or a try for goal occurs, be alert for possible fouls and decide immediately when they occurred in reference to the tap or try. If the foul is by the tapper, the shooter or a teammate, the key is whether it occurred before or after the ball was in flight. If the foul is by an opponent, the decision hinges on whether it occurred

- before the tapping or trying motion started,
- during the tapping or trying motion, or
- after the ball was in flight.

If the foul occurred before the tapping or trying motion began, the ball is dead immediately. If the foul occurred during the attempt or after the ball was in flight, the goal counts if it goes in. If the foul happened after the ball was in flight and was not against the shooter or tapper, administer the penalty regardless of whether the try was successful.

If there is doubt as to whether a successful free throw or field goal is to count, the covering official should signal whether the goal counts. If it counts, make a driving motion with one hand to demonstrate the ball going through the basket (see figure 3.26, a and b). If it does not count, use the prescribed signal (see figure 3.27, a and b).

FIGURE 3.26   *(a and b)* Official signaling the goal counts.

FIGURE 3.27   *(a and b)* Official signaling no score.

Three-Point Tries

When you are the covering official and you anticipate an attempt at a
three-point field goal, position yourself so you can clearly see whether
the attempt comes from behind the arc. When the shot goes up and you
judge that it is indeed a three-point attempt, extend either arm at head
level with three fingers extended (see figure 3.28). If the shot is good, fully
extend both arms over your head with the palms facing each other (see
figure 3.29). The trail official should echo the three-point made signal.

FIGURE 3.28   Official signaling a
three-point attempt.

FIGURE 3.29   Official signaling a successful three-point goal.

For a three-point field goal to be successful, the shooter must have been airborne from behind the three-point line or have his or her foot or feet on the floor behind the line when he or she attempted the shot. If a shooter's foot touches on or inside the line, the shooter is in the two-point area. The position of the shooter bears no relation to the plane.

Last-Second Shot

In a two-person crew, the trail official is responsible for ruling on a last-second shot; in a three-person crew, either the trail official or the center official opposite the table is responsible. On a fast break, the lead official should be ready to assist if asked by the responsible official. The referee makes the final decision in disagreements between officials or if it is necessary to consult the timer.

Be alert for a tap or try for a field goal in the closing seconds. When play is resumed with a throw-in or free throw and three-tenths of a second or less are on the clock, no field goal may be scored by a try for goal. A tap, however, can score. This does not apply if the clock does not display tenths of a second.

The expiration of time always kills the ball immediately, unless time expires after the ball is in flight for a tap or try. In that case, the ball remains live and the period does not end until the tap or try ends. Be aware of the remaining time in a period and watch for the timer's signal.

Finally, do not consult the timer on a last-second tap or try unless you do not hear the timer's signal or the signaling was defective. If it is necessary to consult the timer, the decision remains the referee's. If there is still disagreement as to whether the ball was in flight or contact occurred before the ball became dead, the referee makes the final decision. The timer should watch the ball and another courtside or table person should watch the clock and count aloud the remaining seconds to help the timer.

Communicating With Crewmates

In every game you officiate, you communicate a significant amount of information to the coaches, players, other officials and fans. Much of your communication is accomplished through signaling, but you also communicate verbally. In chapters 1 and 2 we discussed verbal communication with players and coaches. Now we'll focus on communicating with crewmates for help calls, double whistles and changing calls.

Help Calls

Even though you strive to get the best angle at all times, sometimes the action happens so quickly that you don't have time to get in the best position to see the play. When this happens, you may have to rely on a crewmate to help you make the call. Here are some common examples of when you'll need help:

- *Ball tapped out of bounds.* When a ball goes out of bounds and one or more players on both sides touched the ball at about the same time, you have a tough call to make, especially if you're screened by one of the players. Even if the action occurs in your area, you might need help from another official to make the call.
- *Tipped shots.* Another tough call is a shot tipped by a rebounder in or near the cylinder. Know the rules and watch tapes so you know when a basket should be awarded and when interference has occurred, and be ready to call on a crewmate if your vision of the play was hindered.
- *Ball going into the backcourt.* If the ball is advanced into the frontcourt and touched by a defender before it returns to the backcourt, has a violation occurred against the offense? This is the kind of question facing officials.

Double Whistles

Sometimes officials are watching the same players, particularly during on-ball coverage in half-court settings. If two or three officials blow their whistles at the same time, the first thing to do is raise your arm in the air with either your palm or fist, depending on the nature of the call. Make eye contact with your partners before signaling anything else. You will need to conference with the other officials to find out what each of you saw. In most cases, the official toward whom the play is moving takes the call. An exception is if a foul or violation occurred before the partner's whistle.

For example, let's say two whistles sound and both officials raise the appropriate signal to stop the clock. "I've got a charge," says the lead official. "I got a travel before the charge," says the trail official. The lead official lowers his or her arm and the trail official takes the call because the travel happened before the charge. The trail official then signals the traveling violation. Good communication and quick movement prevent embarrassing situations and keep the game moving at a good pace. Disciplined signals and frequent eye contact eliminate double (or triple) calls on double (or triple) whistles.

Changing Calls

You might occasionally need to offer information to your partner for the good of the game. Changing a call is not about ego; it's about accuracy. The overriding goal of the officiating team is getting the call right. Eliminate the word *overrule* from your vocabulary. You are not overruling your partner's call; you are simply attempting to ensure that the correct call is made.

For example, if your partner signals the ball out of bounds on White and you saw Blue touch the ball last, move toward your partner immediately, saying, "Blue touched the ball after White." Don't say, "It looked like Blue touched the ball after White." If you are going to challenge a call, be sure that the information you're offering is correct. After giving your partner the correct information, the official making the original call should signal the change.

If your partner signals a successful three-point goal and you are certain the player's foot was on or inside the three-point arc, blow your whistle and immediately signal two points to the table. To expedite the game, there is no reason to discuss this call. Simply administer the baseline throw-in and continue.

You'll usually only change out-of-bounds calls and three-point attempts. Judgment on fouls and floor violations should almost never be questioned. Don't debate on court about a block or charge. Let the official who made the call live with the decision and then talk about it after the game. Always approach these situations professionally and with a positive, respectful attitude.

Those are the essentials of officiating mechanics. In the next chapter we'll look at similar situations as they apply to two-person crews.

CHAPTER 4

TWO-OFFICIAL MECHANICS

In the previous chapter we covered the general mechanics of officiating. In this chapter we'll focus on the mechanics for two-person crews, and in the next we'll look at mechanics for three-person crews. Chapters 4 and 5 will provide you with all of the mechanics you need to know.

Because most high school games use two-person crews, it's essential that you know how to operate in such a crew. This chapter is integral to your education as an official. It covers the following items:

- Primary coverage areas
- Jump balls
- Throw-ins
- Fouls
- Free throws
- Violations
- Time-outs
- Three-point tries

Primary Coverage Areas

Good mechanics mean at least one official is always in position to clearly see the whole play, so good mechanics begins with understanding the primary coverage areas for a two-person crew. As mentioned in chapter 3, the lead official normally is ahead of the ball on all plays, working four to six feet off the end line, while the trail official is behind the ball on all plays. This section shows the lead and trail officials in on-ball coverage, diagonal court coverage, lead ball-side coverage and delay or four-corner coverage.

On-Ball Coverage

Who has ball coverage depends on where the ball is on the court. For example, in figure 4.1 the lead official has on-ball coverage (shaded area) because that official is near the ball. The trail official is off the ball and covers the rest of the court (lined area). As you can see, the lead official's coverage area extends to the free-throw line and includes the entire free-throw lane.

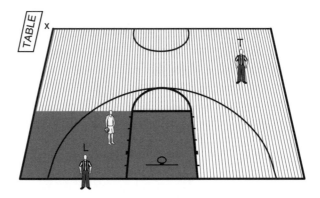

FIGURE 4.1   Areas of responsibility when the lead official has on-ball coverage and the trail official's coverage is off the ball.

If the ball moves outside the lead official's coverage area, the trail official assumes on-ball coverage, and the lead official's coverage is now off the ball (see figure 4.2).

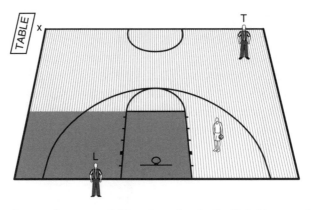

FIGURE 4.2   Areas of responsibility when the trail official has on-ball coverage and the lead official's coverage is off the ball.

If the ball has moved up high near midcourt on the lead official's side, coverage is as shown in figure 4.3. Sometimes an inexperienced lead official thinks that he or she has on-ball coverage in this situation, but the trail official has it, and the lead official has off-ball coverage. Note that the lead official's coverage area extends beyond the free-throw lane; this extended coverage helps the trail official focus on the action surrounding the ball.

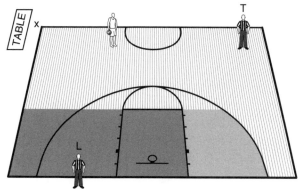

FIGURE 4.3   Lead and trail officials' areas of responsibility when the ball has moved upcourt.

Diagonal Court Coverage

To illustrate diagonal court coverage, we will look at three examples of two officials aligning themselves diagonally across the court.

If the lead official moves into position to cover the ball, the lead official should be ready to make a call on whether a shot in that area is a three-point basket (see figure 4.4). Again, note the lead official's coverage area. The trail official, who is diagonally across from the lead official, covers the significant action off the ball.

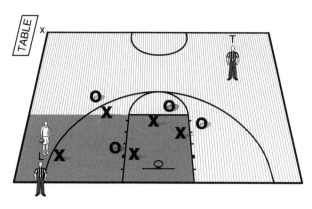

FIGURE 4.4   Lead and trail officials' areas of responsibility when the lead moves to cover the ball near the three-point line.

However, if the ball is out top, as in figure 4.5, the trail official assumes on-ball coverage and must make any calls on shots attempted near the three-point line. The lead official is no longer near the three-point line, but has moved closer to the key. While the trail official has on-ball coverage when the ball is high, the lead official's coverage reaches to the free-throw line extended and the three-point line on the weak side.

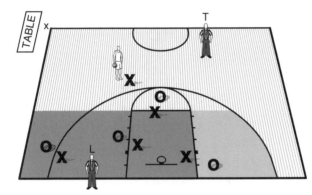

FIGURE 4.5 Lead and trail officials' areas of responsibility when the trail is covering the ball at the top of the circle.

Let's say the ball moves to the weak side, inside the three-point arc (see figure 4.6). In this case, the trail official has on-ball coverage and the lead official moves to the key for off-ball coverage. The two officials maintain diagonal coverage.

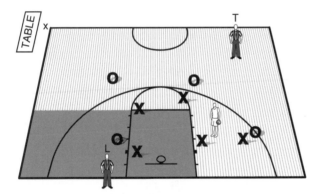

FIGURE 4.6 Lead and trail officials' areas of responsibility when the ball moves to the weak side, inside the three-point arc.

In each of these situations, the officials quickly and smoothly adjust coverage responsibility with minimal yet significant movement. Sometimes the lead official is near the lane line, and sometimes near the three-point line. Likewise, sometimes the trail official is near enough to the three-point line to make a call on an attempt, and sometimes the trail is farther off the line. You need to know how to adjust your positioning, what area of the court you're covering and whether you have on-ball or off-ball coverage. As you gain experience, these adjustments will become more and more seamless.

Lead Ball-Side Coverage

Sometimes diagonal coverage is not the best option. When the post players and the ball move to the same side of the lane as the trail, the lead may have the better angle by moving with them. In such situations the lead official has ball-side coverage.

For example, in figure 4.7 the lead official shifts out of diagonal coverage and moves to the same side of the court as the trail official, who maintains on-ball coverage when the ball is beyond the three-point arc. The lead official rotates to ball-side coverage to be closer to the action. The lead official focuses on off-ball action and tries to maintain a 45-degree angle to the ball.

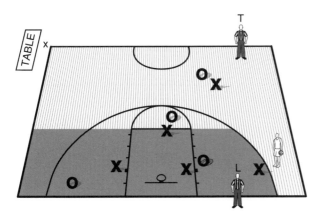

FIGURE 4.7 Lead and trail officials' areas of responsibility when the trail official is on the ball outside the arc and the lead official is ball side and concentrating on action away from the ball.

When the lead and trail officials are on the same side of the lane and the ball goes below the free-throw line extended and inside the arc, the lead official has on-ball coverage (see figure 4.8). The trail official focuses off the ball and helps the lead official by extending coverage into the open area on the opposite side.

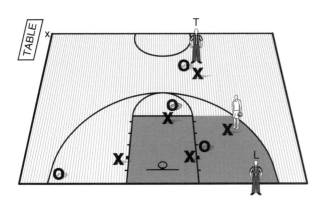

FIGURE 4.8 Lead and trail officials' areas of responsibility when both officials are on the same side of the lane and the ball goes below the free-throw line extended and inside the arc.

If the lead and trail officials are both on the same side when play transitions to the other end of the court, the lead official must remember to return to the other side of the court and resume diagonal coverage (see figure 4.9).

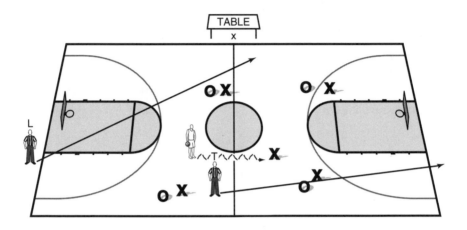

FIGURE 4.9   Lead official resuming diagonal coverage when the play transitions to the other end of the court.

If the ball swings back to the weak side, the lead official should quickly move back across the key to cover the play (see figure 4.10). If a quick shot is put up or the player with the ball drives to the basket, the lead official should close down near the free-throw lane and officiate the play.

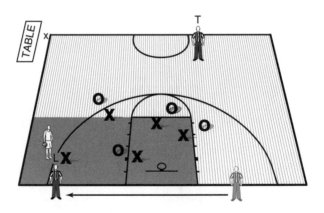

FIGURE 4.10   Lead official covering a play when the ball swings back to the weak side.

Delay or Four-Corner Coverage

When a team goes into a four-corner or delay offense, the officials need to move to the areas indicated in figure 4.11. The trail official moves behind the delay offense, while the lead official moves around the corner to observe lateral movement and watch for contact.

If the corner player on the lead side, or strong side, drives to the basket, the lead official can cut across the corner to observe the action near the basket (see figure 4.12).

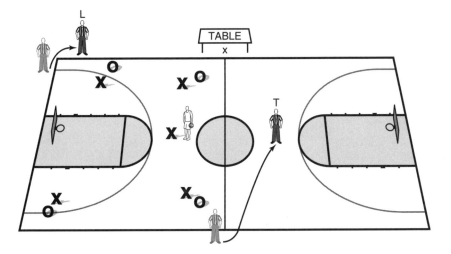

FIGURE 4.11   Lead and trail officials' areas of responsibility when a team goes into a four-corner or delay offense.

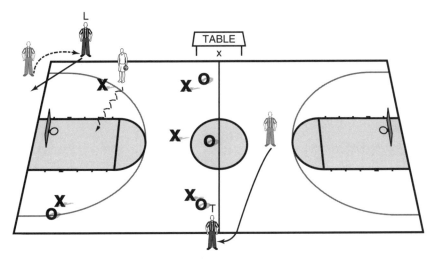

FIGURE 4.12   Lead official's movement when a corner player on the lead side drives to the basket.

Jump Balls

FIGURE 4.13   Correct jump-ball location.

When a jump ball is about to take place, the referee should notify the captain of each team. The referee should make eye contact with each captain and ask if they are ready. A jump ball always takes place in the center restraining circle (see figure 4.13). As the players come onto the court and get into position, each official should count the players on both teams.

The positioning of the two officials is as shown in figure 4.14. The referee is in the center circle, facing the scorer's table, while the umpire is near the division and boundary lines, facing the referee. If you are the umpire, make sure you don't block the scorer's and timer's view of the referee. The umpire is responsible for the actions of the nonjumpers.

The umpire should make sure the clock is set to start the quarter and ask the timer if he or she is ready to go. When a player legally touches

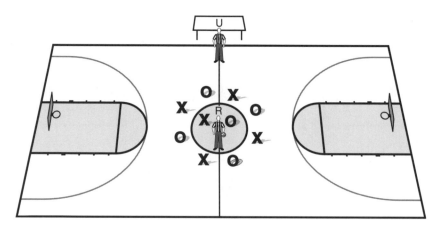

FIGURE 4.14   Referee and umpire positioning for jump balls.

the ball the umpire signals to start the clock (see figure 4.15, a and b). After the tip, the umpire normally moves to become the lead official toward the direction the ball will be moving. If the team gains possession of the ball in their backcourt, the umpire assumes the trail position (see figure 4.16). If the team gains possession of the ball in their frontcourt, the umpire assumes the lead position (see figure 4.17).

FIGURE 4.15 *(a and b)* Umpire signaling to start the clock after the jump ball.

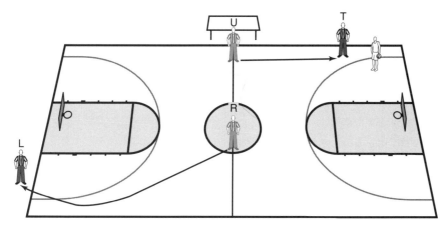

FIGURE 4.16 Umpire assuming trail position when a team gains possession of the ball in their backcourt.

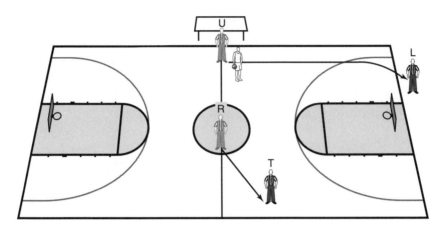

FIGURE 4.17   Umpire assuming lead position when a team gains possession of the ball in their frontcourt.

These are general guidelines that do not cover every play. Officials should discuss any unusual situations that may occur to start the game.

Since the referee must freeze after tossing the ball until the players clear the center circle, the umpire has to get to a position to officiate violations and fouls. Once the umpire has committed to one direction or the other, the referee fills in.

Once ball control, direction of play and initial official positioning are determined, the trail official should check to make sure the possession arrow has been set correctly. Each official covers the nearest sideline, division line and end line.

Throw-Ins

Your responsibilities during throw-ins are dictated by the type of throw-in. In this section we'll cover four types of throw-ins:

- Frontcourt throw-ins
- Backcourt throw-ins
- Throw-ins during a press
- Throw-ins after a technical foul

Frontcourt Throw-Ins

Throw-ins from the frontcourt are administered by the official responsible for the boundary where the throw-in occurs. The lead official is responsible for the end line and the nearest sideline, and the trail official is responsible for the nearest sideline and the division line. The official not administering the throw-in should be positioned so that both sidelines and the end line can be covered. Note the diagonal coverage on the court (see figure 4.18).

If the designated spot for the throw-in is above the free-throw line extended, the lead official who administers the throw-in becomes the trail official (see figure 4.19). If the designated spot is below the free-throw line extended, the lead remains on the end line and bounces the ball to the thrower (see figure 4.20).

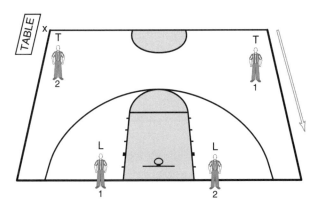

FIGURE 4.18   Positioning for the official not administering the throw-in.

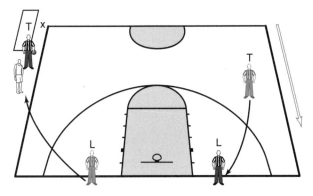

FIGURE 4.19   Lead official (who becomes the new trail) administering a throw-in above the free-throw line extended.

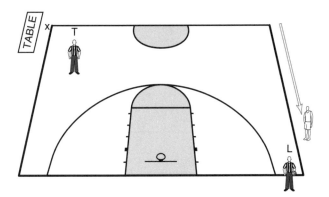

FIGURE 4.20   Lead official administering a sideline throw-in below the free-throw line extended.

Another type of frontcourt throw-in takes place on the sidelines and is administered by the trail official, as shown in figure 4.21. In this figure the officials are using the boxing-in principle, where an official is on each side of the thrower, either on opposite sides of the court or a side and end of the court depending on where the ball will be put in play.

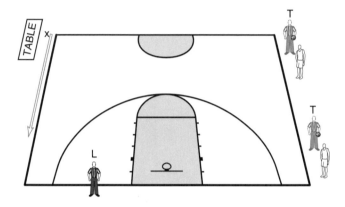

FIGURE 4.21   Trail official administering a frontcourt throw-in on the sidelines.

Backcourt Throw-Ins

The trail official administers all throw-ins in the backcourt while the lead official covers diagonally down the court (see figure 4.22). Both officials maintain responsibility for the sideline and end line or division line that they are responsible for at the time of the throw-in. The trail official holds the ball until the lead official is in position so that the sidelines, end line and division line are adequately covered.

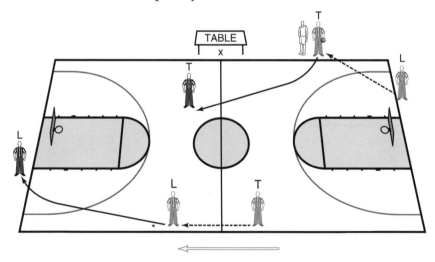

FIGURE 4.22   Trail and lead official maintaining diagonal coverage after a throw-in from the backcourt.

The trail official may bounce the ball to a player inbounding the ball on the end line or the sideline in the backcourt (see figure 4.23). In either case, the trail official administers the throw-in once the lead official is in place in the frontcourt.

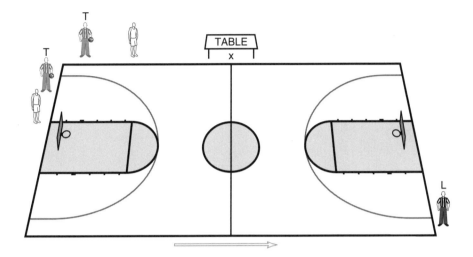

FIGURE 4.23   Trail official in position for a backcourt throw-in on the end line or on the sideline.

Throw-Ins During a Press

Should the defense press on a throw-in, the lead official should be positioned according to the players' location. Start in backcourt and move as play dictates (see figure 4.24).

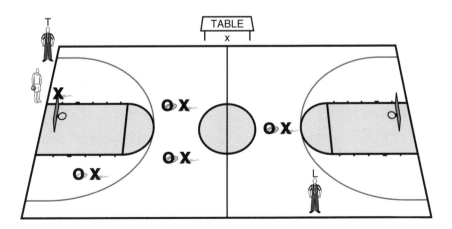

FIGURE 4.24   Lead and trail official positioning in a press situation.

Officials must anticipate the players' movements on a press in order to maintain an angle. However, the lead official should also be in position to beat the play to the baseline on a long pass or fast break.

Throw-Ins After a Technical Foul

When a technical foul is called, officials switch ends of the court as with every other foul. After the lead official administers the free throws, the trail official administers the throw-in at the division line on the side of the court opposite the table (see figure 4.25). Technical fouls often stir up the emotions of players and coaches. Officials might need to adjust their position to keep the calling official away from the coach.

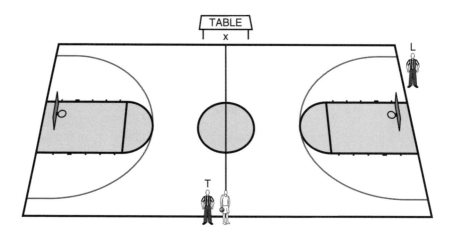

FIGURE 4.25   Trail official positioning for a throw-in after a technical foul.

Fouls

The general mechanics for calling a foul were described in chapter 3 (see pages 41-44). In addition to those mechanics, you are responsible for the following procedures when operating in a two-person crew.

Free Official

If you are the free official, carefully watch all the players until your partner has reported the foul in the foul-reporting area (see figure 4.26) and turned away from the table back to the court and can once again also help observe players. Ignore the ball during the foul report. You and your partner should never turn your back on the players at the same time; the players should always be under complete visual supervision (see "Staying Alert").

If you are the reporting official, move around the players, not between them. Following the report, the free (nonreporting) official secures the ball and gets in position for the free throw or throw-in. Make sure the correct player goes to the line for the free throw.

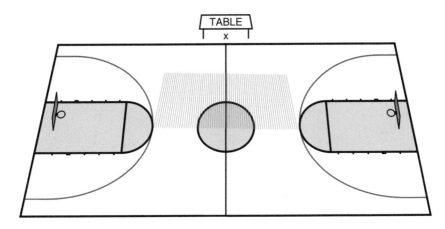

FIGURE 4.26   Foul-reporting area.

Staying Alert

Sometimes an inexperienced official takes a mental break right after a foul has been committed—after all, there's a break in the action, and the crew has been working hard.

However, this is not the time to take a mental break. Players' tempers can easily flare after a foul, and fights don't happen only in close games or after hard fouls. While your crewmate is reporting the foul, the players have time on their hands and are mingling on the court. A brush of the shoulder or a verbal jab can quickly escalate into something physical. Keep a close eye on the players and be ready to squelch any minor argument before it becomes major. This type of preventive officiating is just as important as your ability to make calls and execute mechanics.

Change ends of the court with your crewmate after each foul. The free official should instigate the change before putting the ball in play. For an example of the sequence of a lead official calling a foul, see figure 4.27, a through e.

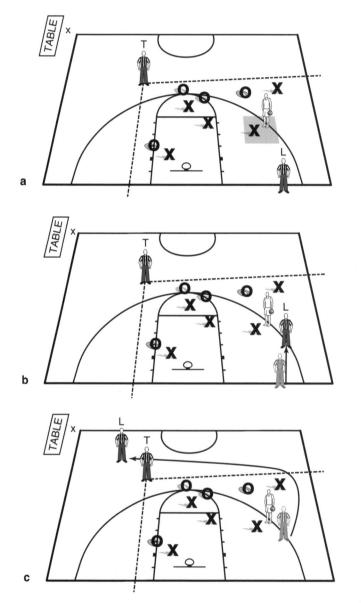

(continued)

FIGURE 4.27   When a foul is called, the trail official *(a)* freezes his or her field of vision and *(b)* observes all players while the lead official *(c)* moves to the reporting area, *(d)* observes the benches and reports the foul to the table. After the report, *(e)* the previous lead official becomes the trail and the previous trail official becomes the lead.

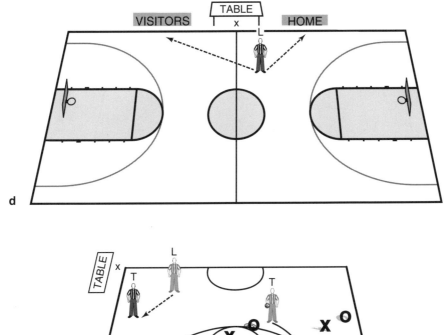

d

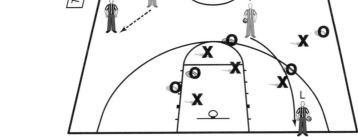

e

FIGURE 4.27 *(continued)*

Free Throws

To administer free throws, both officials in the two-person crew must remember to make eye contact with each other and visually signal to each other the number of free throws. Make sure that the lane spaces are properly occupied. Take a final look at the table before administering the free throw.

The lead official visually and verbally indicates to the players the number of throws, bounces the ball to the thrower, and backs out of the lane. The lead stands about four feet from the nearest lane line, about three feet off the end line and also watches the opposite lane line plus the first space on the side of the scorer's table (see figure 4.28). For more information on mechanics during a free throw, refer to pages 44 through 45 in chapter 3.

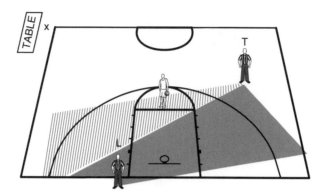

FIGURE 4.28   Lead and trail officials' responsibilities and areas of coverage for a free throw.

The trail official should assume the standard free-throw position, just behind the free-throw line extended and halfway between the near free-throw lane and the sideline (see figure 4.28). In addition, the trail official checks the position of the thrower's feet and begins the visible count using a wrist flick, being careful not to distract the shooter. As the trail official, you should also do the following:

- Continue to observe the thrower's feet in relation to the free-throw line and watch for a violation by the thrower.
- Observe the top three spaces on the opposite lane line for violations and immediately give the appropriate signal when either team violates.
- Step toward the end line when the thrower releases the ball.
- Watch the flight of the ball and note whether it goes through, contacts or misses the ring.
- Watch the rebounding action, keeping an eye out for goaltending or basket interference.
- Signal to start the clock if the final throw or the first throw of a one-and-one is unsuccessful and the ball remains live.

Free Throw After Technical Foul

After a technical foul, administer the free throws with no players along the lane. The lead official administers the free throws while the trail official moves to the best position for supervision. Following the second free throw, the lead official bounces the ball to the trail official, who goes to the division line on the side of the court opposite the table and administers the throw-in (see figure 4.25 on page 68).

Free Throw After Intentional or Flagrant Foul

After an intentional or flagrant personal foul, no players are allowed along the lane for the free throws. The lead official administers both free throws while the trail official moves to the best position for supervision. The throw-in occurs at the out-of-bounds spot nearest to where the foul occurred. The official responsible for the line from where the throw-in is to take place administers the throw-in.

Violations

When you are in a two-person crew and you note basket interference or goaltending, stop the clock or keep it stopped. Report to the scorer if he or she might not be sure how many points should be awarded.

The trail official is responsible for observing basket interference or goaltending, although in some situations the lead official, who is responsible for action under the basket, is in position to call goaltending or basket interference. Mechanics for calling violations were covered in chapter 3 (see pages 45-47).

Time-Outs

When you grant a time-out, report the shirt color and number of the player or the coach who requested the time-out. After you have sounded your whistle and signaled to stop the clock, inform the players of the time-out and observe them moving to their bench area, then move to the reporting area. As you do, ask the coach if a 30-second or 60-second time-out is being requested. All officials should immediately give the 30-second or 60-second time-out signal (see figures 4.29 and 4.30, a and b). Report the time-out by saying, "thirty-second (or sixty-second) time-out, called by Red thirty-two. Start the timer." If the coach signaled for the time-out, indicate this by forming a "C" with your hand.

FIGURE 4.29   Official signaling a 30-second time-out.

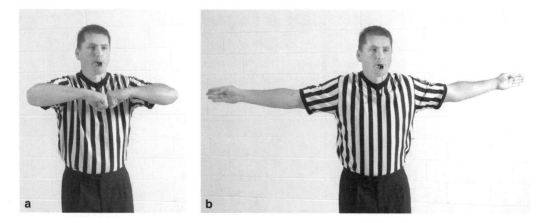

FIGURE 4.30   *(a and b)* Official signaling a 60-second time-out.

During any time-out, maintain good posture and stay alert. During a 30-second time-out, stand at the top of the arc. During a 60-second time-out, each official takes a position on the nearest block (neutral zone), opposite and facing the scorer's table (see figure 4.31).

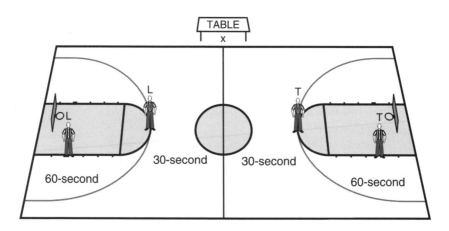

FIGURE 4.31   Lead and trail officials' positioning for 30- and 60-second time-outs.

If you are the official who will administer the throw-in following a time-out, secure the ball. Be ready to indicate the throw-in spot to both coaches. The official administering the throw-in can indicate the direction the ball is going to be put in play by holding the ball in front, back or to the side of the body in the direction the team with the throw-in is going. Both officials should be ready to use the proper signal to beckon substitutes into the game (see figure 4.32, a and b) and to give the scorer and timer any information they request.

During the intermission between quarters, take the same positions as shown in figure 4.31 for a 60-second time-out. The referee should be on the block (neutral zone) in the backcourt of the team entitled to the throw-in. Don't talk to your crewmate unless you need to discuss a game situation. Both officials are responsible for counting the players on each team as they enter the court. On a throw-in following an intermission, the administering official sounds the whistle before handing the ball to the thrower, indicating that play is about to begin.

a   b

FIGURE 4.32   *(a and b)* Official beckoning a substitute into the game.

Three-Point Tries

Mechanics for three-point attempts and shots were covered in chapter 3 on pages 51 through 52. However, when you are the trail official in a two-person crew and you are covering a three-point attempt (figures 4.33 and 4.34), there is no need for the lead official to mirror your signal of a successful attempt. On the other hand, if you are the lead official and you signal a successful three-point shot (see figure 4.35), the trail official *should* mirror your signal. In any case, don't turn your back on the players and the court when you're signaling.

Study chapters 3 and 4 as well as the *NFHS Basketball Rules Book* to learn the mechanics for a two-person crew. Your understanding of the mechanics and your ability to execute them are keys to your success as an official. In the next chapter we'll look at mechanics for a three-person crew.

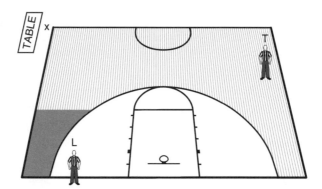

FIGURE 4.33   Lead and trail officials' areas of responsibility on a three-point attempt.

FIGURE 4.34   Trail official signaling a three-point attempt.

FIGURE 4.35   Official signaling a successful three-point shot.

CHAPTER 5

Three-Official Mechanics

While fans might think it's easier to officiate in a three-person crew, you still have to be in the right position and know the mechanics of operating with three officials on the court—not easy when you're probably used to working in a two-person crew. Knowing how to operate in a three-person crew is essential for any official.

There are many advantages to using three officials, the greatest of which is improved coverage. Always having an official in position and an extra set of eyes watching can deter fouling and therefore promote better basketball.

The primary responsibilities of each official are detailed in this chapter. We'll explore issues such as basic principles, primary coverage areas, throw-ins, fouls, violations, time-outs and more.

Basic Principles

A three-person crew consists of a lead official, center official and trail official. In this section we'll examine the basic principles of officiating in such a crew, including general positioning and triangle coverage.

General Positioning

In this section we'll address the general positioning of the lead, center (C) and trail officials. For the main coverage areas see figure 5.1.

While a two-person crew often maintains diagonal court coverage, a three-person crew maintains wide triangle coverage. Each official is responsible for an area of coverage that remains the same on and off the ball. Always be aware of the location of the ball, the players and your crewmates, and never turn your back to the court. All officials call plays that they clearly see, regardless of whether the plays occur in their area of responsibility.

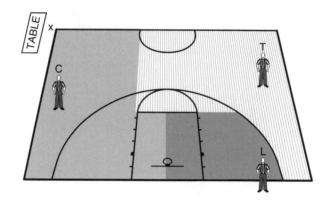

FIGURE 5.1   Primary coverage areas for the lead, center and trail officials.

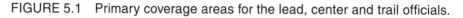

Benefits of a Three-Official Crew

A three-person crew can use a wide triangle formation to improve court coverage in both the frontcourt and backcourt. They can also treat both sides of the court the same in regard to primary areas of coverage. In addition, they

- have more clearly defined areas of coverage and responsibility,
- provide more effective coverage in press and full-court situations,
- strengthen the philosophy of strong-side officiating by allowing the lead and trail officials to officiate the ball and the players that are between them, and
- improve off-ball coverage through the center official, who is responsible for off-ball screens, backside coverage and weak-side rebounding.

Lead Official

When you are lead official, you assume an initial position of depth, generally four to six feet, off the end line and take end-line responsibility. You are on the trail official's side, though you adjust your position according to ball position between the lane extended and the arc (see figure 5.2)—you move between those two areas while staying off the end line.

FIGURE 5.2   Lead official's adjusted positioning between the lane-line extended and the arc.

Center Official

When you are the center official, you take an initial position in line with the free-throw line extended and have sideline responsibility from end line to end line (see figure 5.3). You remain the center official on the other end of the court when the ball initially changes possession, though your position might change later on.

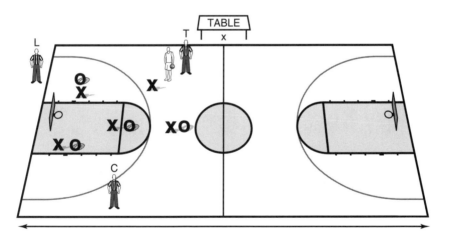

FIGURE 5.3   Center official taking an intitial position in line with the free-throw line extended, with sideline responsibility from end line to end line.

Trail Official

As trail official, you take an intitial position about 28 feet from the end line, near the top of the three-point arc and the sideline. You have division-line and sideline responsibility from end line to end line. Your depth of coverage in the frontcourt is dictated by game action. When the ball is between the division line and the 28-foot mark, you should move toward midcourt to get an angle between the players. Once the ball goes below the 28-foot mark, you close down, or if a shot is taken, you must be prepared to close down around the 28-foot mark (see figure 5.4).

FIGURE 5.4   Trail official's positioning at the top of the three-point arc, with division-line and sideline responsibility from end to end.

Two other matters of note for a three-person crew:

- When a team employs a delay or spread offense, all officials should maintain normal officiating positions and responsibilities.
- When the ball goes out of bounds and the responsible official needs help, look to the official sharing that area of responsibility, who should be prepared to give assistance.

Primary Coverage Areas

In this section we'll examine the primary coverage area of each official for the following:

- Ball movement and basic rotation
- Transition coverage
- Shot and rebound coverage
- Three-point tries
- Press

Ball Movement and Basic Rotation

The movement of the ball determines the movement of the officials. For example, figure 5.5 shows the movement of the officials based on the ball's movement. As the ball swings from one side of the court to the other, the

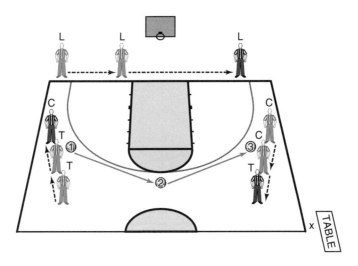

FIGURE 5.5   Ball determining the movement of the officials.

lead moves with the ball from one side of the lane to the other, and the trail and the center rotate positions. The trail official becomes the center official, picking up primary coverage off the ball, and the center official becomes the trail official on the strong side.

As the ball swings to the center of the court, the lead official closes down near the lane line. The lead moves across the lane and rotates when the ball penetrates the free-throw lane line extended nearest the center official. The exception to this is a quick shot or a drive to the basket. When a player with the ball starts a drive to the basket from an official's primary area, that official has the player and the ball all the way to the basket.

A few final notes on covering ball movement and the basic rotation:

- The lead official is responsible for players in the post even as he or she is moving across the lane.
- In most situations, the lead official moves to the ball side of the court. Sometimes, because of a quick swing pass, a skip pass or a shot, the lead will not have time to move ball side.
- There may be two center officials at once as rotation is occurring, but there should rarely be two trail officials at once.

Transition Coverage

When a turnover or change of possession takes place, the lead official and trail official switch duties. The center official always remains the center in transition coverage. See figure 5.6 for an example of transition coverage.

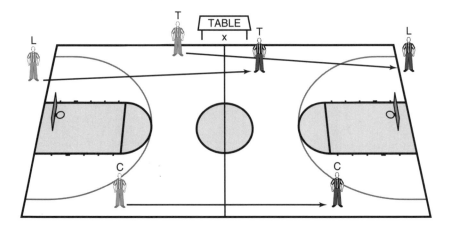

FIGURE 5.6   Transition coverage.

On a fast break or when a quick outlet pass occurs, the new trail official assumes responsibility for sideline coverage (see figure 5.7). This gives the new lead official time to adjust while moving into position on the end line. Never turn your back to the ball when changing direction.

As the fast break develops, the new lead official takes the ball. The new trail official stays with the player who passed the ball, covering the backside of the fast break. The trail official maintains a pace to trail the play up the court. The center official moves up the court and assumes the center position on the other end. The new lead official might initiate a rotation when all three officials are finally in the frontcourt.

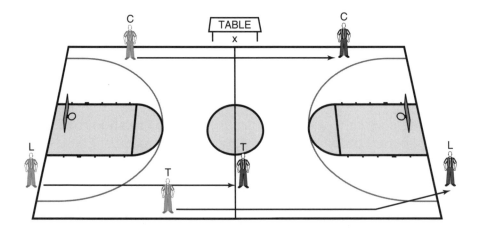

FIGURE 5.7   Trail official assuming responsibility for the sideline.

Shot and Rebound Coverage

In anticipation of a made basket, officials often bail out of their rebounding responsibilities and head for the other end of the floor. However, even a good shooting team only makes 30 to 40 percent of their attempts. The trail and center officials must hold their position or step toward the baseline when each shot is taken and focus on their rebounding responsibilities. Depending on where the shot is taken, the officials must watch strong-side, weak-side and perimeter rebounding. In this section we'll focus on shot and rebound coverage for shots coming from the following areas:

- Near the foul line
- Lead official's area
- Trail official's area
- Center official's area

Near the Foul Line

The trail official is responsible for all shots and resultant rebound action in the foul-line half-circle. The center official helps the trail official with shots from the foul-line half-circle on the center official's side. See figure 5.8 for the trail and center officials' areas of responsibility on shots around the free-throw line.

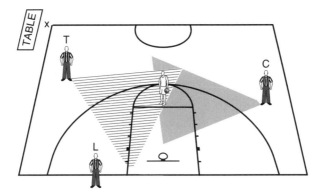

FIGURE 5.8 Trail and center officials' areas of responsibility on shots around the free-throw line.

Lead Official's Area

When the shot comes from the lead official's area (see figure 5.9, a and b), the lead official has the shooter and strong-side rebounding action. The center official has interference and goaltending as well as weak-side rebounding. The trail official has interference and goaltending in addition to perimeter rebounding.

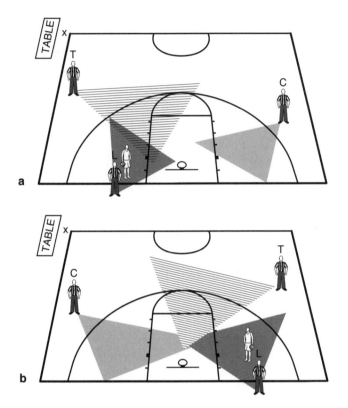

a

b

FIGURE 5.9   Officials' coverage of a shot and rebound from the lead's *(a)* left and *(b)* right.

Trail Official's Area

On shots from the trail official's area, the trail official has the shooter and the three-point line and then covers interference, goaltending and the perimeter rebound. The lead official has the strong-side rebound, and the center official has interference, goaltending and the weak-side rebound (see figure 5.10).

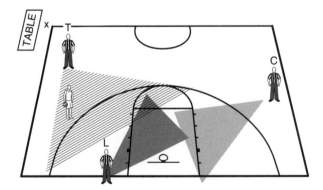

FIGURE 5.10   Officials' coverage of a shot and rebound from the trail official's area.

Center Official's Area

On shots coming from the center official's area, the center official has the shooter and the three-point line and covers interference, goaltending and the weak-side rebound. The lead official has the strong-side rebound, and the trail official has interference, goaltending and the perimeter rebound (see figure 5.11).

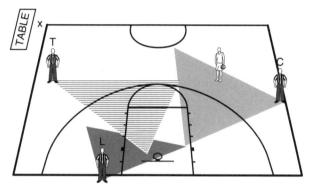

FIGURE 5.11   Officials' coverage of a shot and rebound from the center's area.

Three-Point Tries

On three-point tries, only the covering official should indicate the attempt (see figure 5.12). The indication should be made with the arm closest to the center of the court. The covering official also signals if the attempt is successful. If the trail official signals a successful three-point shot (see figure 5.13), the center official mirrors the successful signal, and vice versa.

FIGURE 5.12   Official signaling a three-point attempt.

FIGURE 5.13   Official signaling a successful three-point shot.

The lead official usually is not responsible for indicating a three-point attempt. However, the lead must be prepared to assist on a fast break or a shot in the corner. See figure 5.14 for the trail and center officials' areas of responsibility on a three-point attempt.

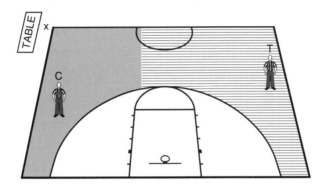

FIGURE 5.14   Trail and center officials' areas of responsibility on a three-point attempt.

Press

In press situations when all the players are in the backcourt, use a wide triangle to keep congested areas covered (see figure 5.15). The lead official becomes the new trail official and has the 10-second count in the backcourt. This official stays with the play action and is alert for the possibility of a turnover. The center and trail officials cover the action in the backcourt, moving with the ball, and the center official assists the trail official with division-line violations. The center official must resist the urge to run upcourt ahead of the pressure.

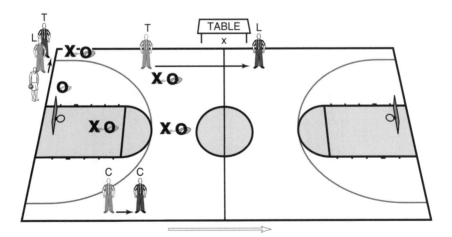

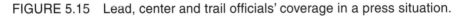

FIGURE 5.15   Lead, center and trail officials' coverage in a press situation.

The new lead official takes a position near the division line and covers quick breaks and long passes. This official stays behind all players; no one is closer to the basket on the other end of the court. Note in figure 5.16 that the new lead official goes deeper into the frontcourt if players are on that end of the court.

All officials should keep moving and avoid being blocked out in press situations.

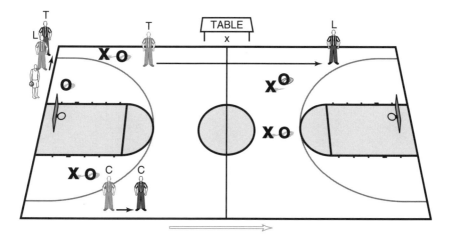

FIGURE 5.16   Lead official's deeper frontcourt positioning in a press situation when players are on the other end of the court.

Jump Balls

Before a jump ball, the referee notifies the captain of each team that play is about to begin. The jump ball always takes place in the center restraining circle. The two umpires, U1 and U2, count the players as they come onto the court. U1 counts the home team and U2 counts the visiting team.

See figure 5.17 for the three officials' positioning. U1 takes a position to the left of the referee, near the sideline on the table side of the court, about 28 feet from the nearest end line. U1 is primarily responsible for the two jumpers, calling back poor tosses and signaling the clock to start when the ball is legally touched.

U2 takes a position about 28 feet from the nearest end line on the side opposite U1. U2 is responsible for the position and action of the nonjumpers.

If a player commits a violation before legal touching, sound your whistle and give the time-out signal to prevent the clock from starting. If there is no violation before a player touches the toss, U1 signals to start the clock when the ball is legally touched (see figure 5.18, a and b). If this

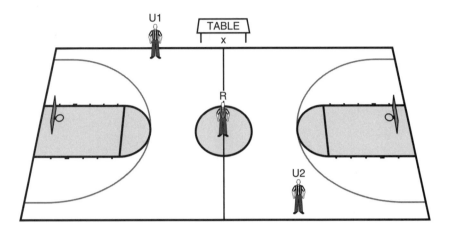

FIGURE 5.17   Officials' positioning for a jump ball.

FIGURE 5.18   *(a and b)* U1 signaling to start the clock after the jump ball.

is followed by a violation, such as a jumper catching the ball after it has been touched, stop the clock by sounding your whistle and giving the stop-clock signal (see figure 5.19).

FIGURE 5.19   U1 signaling to stop the clock when a violation occurs after a jump ball.

The two free officials should be ready to move in either direction, keeping in mind the ball could change direction quickly. When the ball goes to the referee's right, U2 becomes the lead official and U1 becomes the center official (see figure 5.20a). The referee holds position until the players clear and then moves to the position of trail official. While moving into position, check the table to see that the arrow has been set correctly. The lead official should be ready to rule on a quick three-point try.

When the ball goes to the referee's left, U1 becomes the lead official and U2 becomes the center official (see figure 5.20b). Again, the referee holds position until the players clear and then becomes the trail official and checks the directional arrow to see that it is correct.

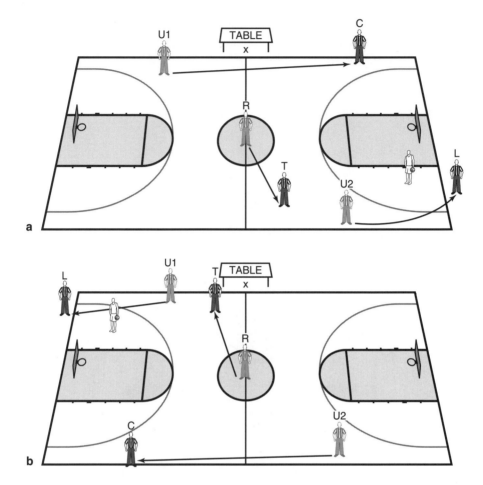

FIGURE 5.20   Officials' positioning when a jump ball goes to the referee's *(a)* right and *(b)* left.

Throw-Ins

The lead official handles throw-ins only on the end line in the frontcourt. The trail official handles all throw-ins in the backcourt. The official that calls a violation should indicate the throw-in spot. Following are the mechanics for throw-ins in the frontcourt and backcourt.

Frontcourt Throw-In

The lead official is responsible for covering the entire end line, the trail official is responsible for the entire sideline on the near side of the court and the division line, and the center official is responsible for the entire sideline on his or her side of the court (see figure 5.21). Whatever official

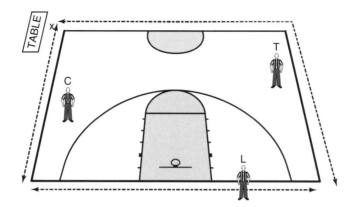

FIGURE 5.21   Lead, trail and center officials' areas of coverage for throw-ins in the frontcourt.

you are, you should not be stationary; move to get proper coverage. If you are the lead official, position yourself four to six feet from the end line to gain a wider view of play in that area.

Frontcourt Throw-In on the End Line

In frontcourt throw-ins on the end line, the lead official has the option of being between the ball and the basket or between the ball and the sideline. If you are the lead official, base your position on what will provide the best coverage. Figure 5.22 shows official positions for a frontcourt end-line throw-in on the side opposite the table, and figure 5.23 shows positions for a similar throw-in on the table side.

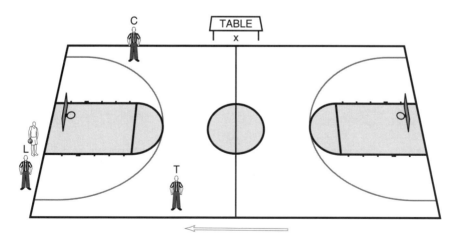

FIGURE 5.22   Lead, trail and center officials' positioning for an opposite-side frontcourt throw-in on the end line.

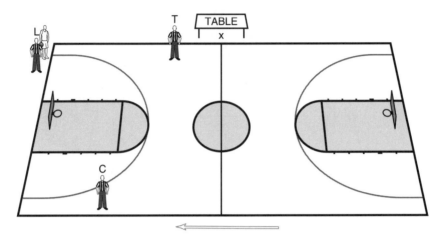

FIGURE 5.23   Lead, trail and center officials' positioning for a table-side front-court throw-in.

Frontcourt Throw-In on the Sideline

Figure 5.24 shows the center official becoming the new trail official and administering a throw-in on the sideline, opposite the table. The trail official becomes the new center official and moves into position in the frontcourt near the free-throw line extended and the sideline, and the lead official moves across the lane to box in the play. Remember, on this and on all sideline throw-ins bounce the ball to the player throwing in.

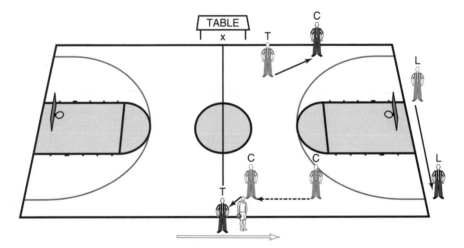

FIGURE 5.24   Center official becoming the trail official and administering a frontcourt sideline throw-in opposite the table.

Backcourt Throw-In

The trail official administers throw-ins from the backcourt. As with frontcourt throw-ins, the center official is responsible for the entire sideline on the near side of the court. The lead official takes a position off the end line and adjusts to the players as the play proceeds. As with all other throw-ins, you won't be stationary; continue to move to get the best angle for coverage.

Backcourt Throw-In on the End Line

The trail official handles the throw-in, taking a position between the ball and the nearer sideline. The center official is near the division line, adjusting position to the players and the pressure of the defense. The lead official is in the frontcourt in a spot off the end line, also adjusting position to the players. The ball and all the players must be in the frontcourt before the lead official initiates a rotation. Figure 5.25 shows a backcourt end-line throw-in on the table side; figure 5.26 shows a backcourt end-line throw-in on the side opposite the table.

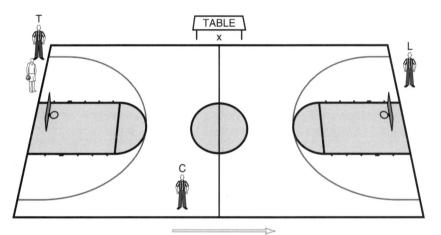

FIGURE 5.25   Lead, trail and center officials' positioning for a backcourt end-line throw-in on the table side.

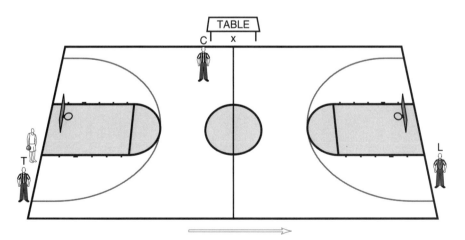

FIGURE 5.26   Lead, trail and center officials' positioning for a backcourt end-line throw-in opposite the table.

Backcourt Throw-In on the Sideline

If the ball goes out of bounds on the trail official's sideline and the play is going long, the old lead official administers the throw-in and becomes the new trail official (see figure 5.27). If the ball goes out on the center official's side and the play is going long, the center official becomes lead official, the trail official becomes center official, and the old lead official who becomes the new trail official handles the throw-in (see figure 5.28).

The trail official takes a position between the ball and the near end line. The center official is near the division line, adjusting to players and pressure, and the lead official is in the home spot off the end line in the frontcourt, also adjusting to the players. All three officials must be in the frontcourt before the lead official initiates any rotation.

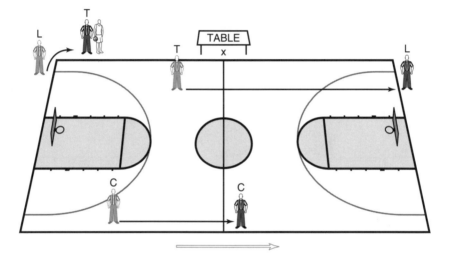

FIGURE 5.27   Ball out of bounds on the trail official's sideline; going long.

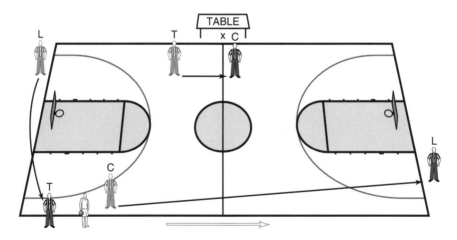

FIGURE 5.28   Ball out of bounds on the center official's sideline; going long.

Fouls

When calling a foul, follow the mechanics detailed in chapter 3. In this section, we'll focus on the duties of the calling official and the noncalling officials and on foul-switching protocol.

Calling Official

If you are the official making the foul call, move quickly to the play and make the call. The foul-calling official goes table side when calling a foul in frontcourt and when calling a foul in backcourt where the fouled player was shooting free throws (see figure 5.29, a and b). When calling a foul in the backcourt and the fouled player is not shooting free throws, the officials slide just as if a violation were called. As you report to the table, make sure you go around the players instead of through them.

Communication with coaches and the officials' table is enhanced when the reporting official remains table side. If a coach has a question about a call, it's better to remain table side if you made the call so the coach doesn't feel compelled to shout across the floor to get your attention. This procedure also shortens the dead-ball period.

FIGURE 5.29 *(a)* Lead official calling a foul with an end-line throw-in, and *(b)* center official calling a foul with a sideline throw-in.

You have the option of going opposite the table if a situation with a coach becomes excessively confrontational (see figure 5.30, a and b). Such situations might occur when calling a disqualifying foul on a player or a technical on a coach. Discuss possible situations with your crewmates during the pregame conference.

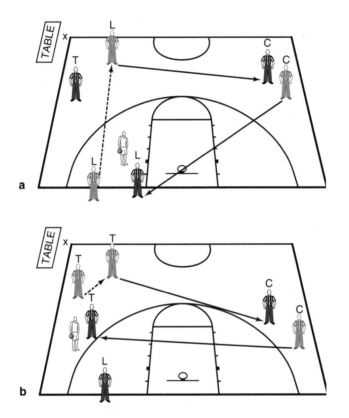

FIGURE 5.30   *(a)* Lead official calling a foul and going opposite, and *(b)* trail official calling a foul and going opposite.

Noncalling Officials

If you are one of the noncalling officials, observe all players as the calling official reports to the table. Ignore the ball while the foul is being reported.

The official who was originally table side usually fills the vacancy left by the calling official. If you are the other noncalling official, you should remain in the position you occupied at the time of the foul. If the calling official was table side to begin with, no switching occurs.

If a foul occurs on a shot and the ball goes in the basket but the calling official has not signaled whether the basket counts, tell the calling official that the ball went in. Do this before the official reports to the table, after which it is the responsibility of the calling official to either count or disallow the basket.

After the reporting official has reported the foul and taken a position table side, the official responsible for administering the throw-in or free throws secures the ball while keeping the players in view and moving to the proper position for the ensuing play. If one or more free throws are to be taken, ensure that the correct free thrower is on the line.

If you are the trail official, it's your duty to notify the coach and then the player of disqualification and to administer substitutions. If you aren't the calling official, move slowly toward your new position as you continue to observe the players.

Switching Positions

Most often, fouls call for two of the three officials to switch positions after the foul has been reported. As mentioned, in most cases the official who was originally table side switches positions with the reporting official.

In some cases, however, officials remain in their position. In this section we'll examine when to remain in the same position and when to switch. As you study each figure, consider not just the mechanics involved but the reason behind them. This will help you learn when to remain in the same position and when to make the appropriate switch.

Lead Official Calls the Foul

As we'll see, switching when the lead official calls a foul depends on the situation.

When the lead official reports a foul in the frontcourt, the ball remains in the frontcourt and no free throws are coming, the officials switch as shown in figure 5.31. After the foul is reported, the lead and trail officials switch positions. The center official remains the center official.

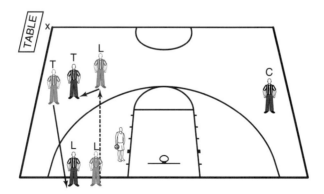

FIGURE 5.31   Lead official calling a foul table side with no free throws.

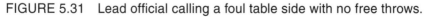

Figure 5.32 shows another situation in which the lead official calls a foul in the frontcourt and the ball remains in the frontcourt with no free throws coming. Because the original center official was table side, the lead and center officials switch positions after the lead official reports the foul. The trail official does not change positions.

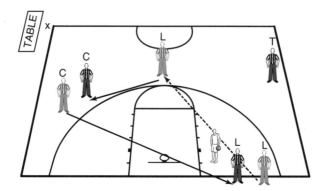

FIGURE 5.32   Lead official calling a foul opposite the table with no free throws.

Figure 5.33 shows a free-throw situation in which the lead official reports a foul and remains table side, switching with the trail official, who becomes the new lead official. The center official does not change positions.

FIGURE 5.33   Lead official calling a foul table side with free throws.

Another free-throw situation is shown in figure 5.34, where the lead reports the foul and remains table side to become the trail official. The center official, who was table side, becomes the new lead official, and the trail official, on the opposite side of the court, becomes the new center official.

FIGURE 5.34   Lead official calling a foul opposite with free throws.

In figure 5.35, the lead calls a foul in the frontcourt, the ball now goes from the backcourt to the frontcourt and there are no free throws. After reporting the foul, the lead official becomes the new trail official, the trail official becomes the new lead official, and the center official stays the same. There is no long switch in this situation.

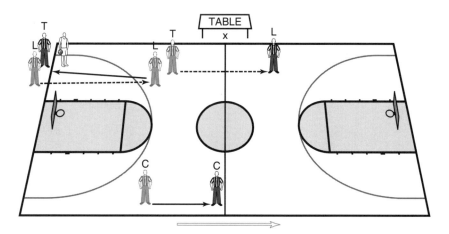

FIGURE 5.35   Lead official calling a foul in the backcourt going long.

Figure 5.36 illustrates another situation involving no free throws. The lead official reports a foul and goes back to the end line to become the trail official. The center official does not change positions. The old trail official becomes the lead official.

In figure 5.37, the lead official reports a foul that results in free throws on the other end of the floor. The lead official then becomes the new trail official. The trail official becomes the new lead official while the center official does not change positions.

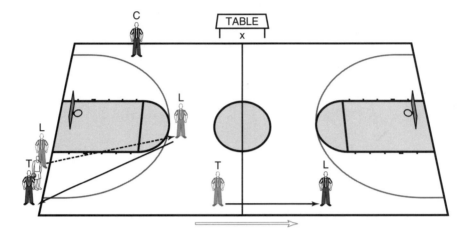

FIGURE 5.36   Lead official calling a foul opposite the table in the backcourt going long.

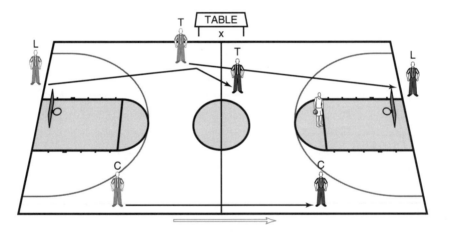

FIGURE 5.37   Lead official calling a foul table side in the backcourt with free throws at the other end.

Figure 5.38 shows the opposite-side lead official calling a foul that results in free throws at the other end. After reporting the foul, the lead official becomes the new trail official and the trail official becomes the new lead official, administering the free throws. The center official moves to the opposite side of the court and remains center official.

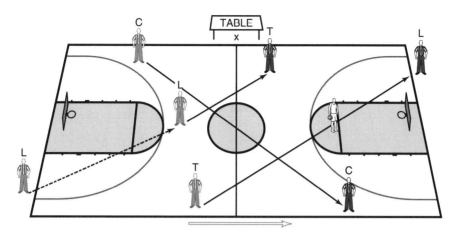

FIGURE 5.38   Lead official calling a foul opposite the table in the backcourt with free throws at the other end.

Center Official Calls the Foul

Many times the center official switches with another official after reporting a foul.

In figure 5.39, the opposite-side center official reports a foul in the frontcourt. The ball remains in the frontcourt but no free throws are awarded. The center official remains center table side. The trail official moves to the opposite side, remaining the trail official, and the lead official remains as lead, moving opposite.

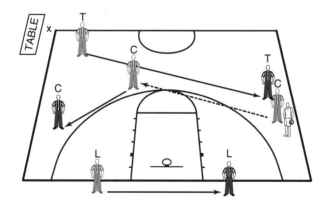
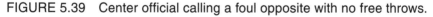

FIGURE 5.39   Center official calling a foul opposite with no free throws.

Figure 5.40 shows another situation in which the table-side center official reports a foul in the frontcourt, the ball remains in the frontcourt and no free throws are awarded. The center official stays table side and becomes the new trail official, and the trail official becomes the new center official, staying on the opposite side. The lead official stays the lead and moves table side.

FIGURE 5.40   Center official calling a foul table side with no free throws.

Figure 5.41 shows a situation in which the table-side center official calls a foul that results in free throws and then becomes the new trail official. The lead official remains the lead, moving table side. The old trail official becomes the center.

FIGURE 5.41   Center official calling a foul table side with free throws.

When the opposite-side center official reports a foul in the frontcourt and the ball is to remain in the frontcourt with free throws awarded, the center moves table side to become the new trail official (see figure 5.42). The trail official moves opposite and becomes the new center official.

Figure 5.43 shows the center official reporting a foul in the backcourt that results in the action moving to the frontcourt, with no free throws awarded. The center official stays table side and becomes the new lead official, the lead official moves table side to become the new trail official, and the trail official becomes the new center official.

FIGURE 5.42 Center official calling a foul opposite the table with free throws.

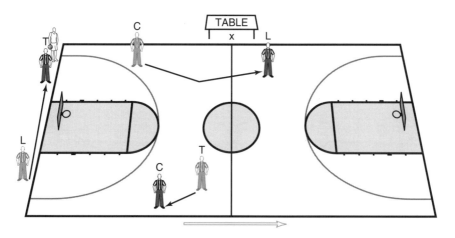

FIGURE 5.43 Center official calling a foul table side in the backcourt going long.

In figure 5.44, the opposite-side center calls and reports an offensive frontcourt foul and becomes the new lead official. The old trail official becomes the new center official, and the old lead official becomes the new trail official and handles the throw-in.

In figure 5.45 the center official calls a backcourt foul and reports it to the table. The action moves to the frontcourt and free throws are awarded. The center official becomes the new trail official, the trail official becomes the new lead official and moves table side, and the lead official becomes the new center official.

Another backcourt foul resulting in free throws at the other end is shown in figure 5.46. The opposite-side center official reports the foul and goes table side to become the new trail official. The trail official becomes the new lead official and administers the free throws. The lead official becomes the new center official, moving to the opposite side.

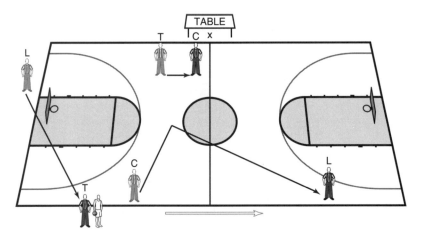

FIGURE 5.44   Center official calling a foul opposite the table in the backcourt going long.

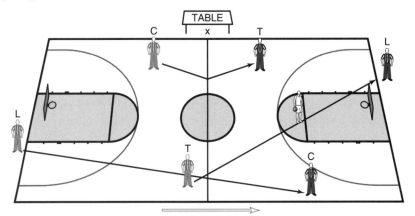

FIGURE 5.45   Center official calling a foul table side in the backcourt with free throws at the other end.

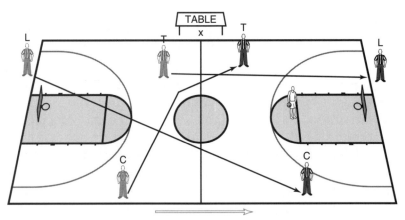

FIGURE 5.46   Center official calling a foul opposite the table in the backcourt with free throws at the other end.

Trail Official Calls the Foul

Following are situations in which the trail official calls the foul and the officials need to switch positions.

In figure 5.47, the opposite-side trail official calls a foul in the front-court that results in a sideline throw-in for the offended team. The trail official moves table side and becomes the new center official. The table-side center official goes opposite and becomes the new trail official and administers the throw-in.

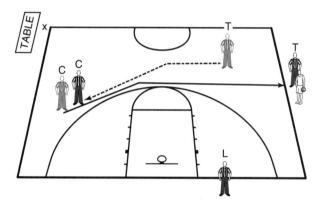

FIGURE 5.47   Trail official calling a foul opposite with no free throws.

Figure 5.48 shows the opposite-side trail official calling and report-ing a foul in the frontcourt that results in a free throw. The trail official moves table side and remains the trail official. The center official moves opposite and remains the center official. The lead official will administer the free throws table side.

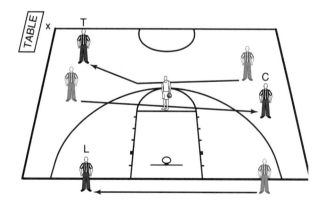

FIGURE 5.48   Trail official calling a foul opposite with free throws.

In figure 5.49, the table-side trail official calls a foul in the backcourt that moves the ball to the other end but does not result in free throws. The trail official remains table side and becomes the new lead official, while the lead official becomes the new trail official and puts the ball in play. The center official does not change positions.

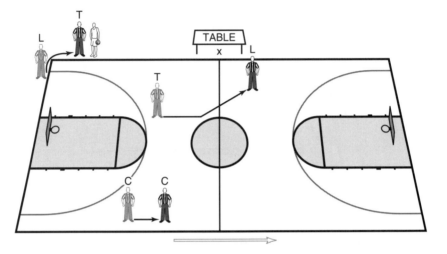

FIGURE 5.49   Trail official calling a foul table side in the backcourt going long.

Figure 5.50 shows the opposite-side trail official calling and reporting an offensive foul in the frontcourt that results in a throw-in for the fouled team. The trail official becomes the new lead official on the other end of the court. The center official does not change positions, and the lead official becomes the new trail official and administers the throw-in.

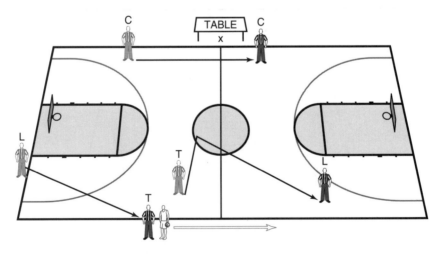

FIGURE 5.50   Trail official calling a foul opposite the table in the backcourt going long.

Figure 5.51 shows the table-side trail official reporting a frontcourt foul that results in free throws at the other end. The trail official remains table side as trail official, while the center and lead officials switch positions as shown. The new lead official administers the free throws.

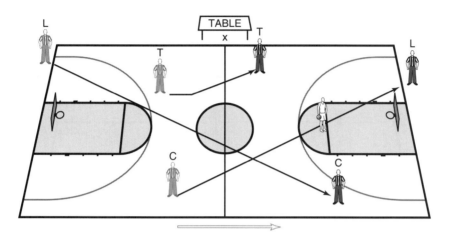

FIGURE 5.51   Trail official calling a foul table side in the backcourt with free throws at the other end.

In figure 5.52, the opposite-side trail official calls a foul in the frontcourt, resulting in free throws at the other end. The trail official goes table side as trail official, while the center and lead officials switch positions, with the new lead official administering the free throws.

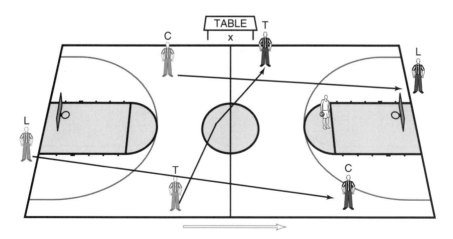

FIGURE 5.52   Trail official calling a foul opposite the table in the backcourt with free throws at the other end.

No Switch

In many situations officials don't switch positions after a foul is called. Many times the officials move down the court but transition as if it were a turnover or violation.

Officials shouldn't switch positions on fouls called in the backcourt that result in play going to the frontcourt and no free throws awarded (see figure 5.53 and 5.54). In these situations officials simply slide down the court.

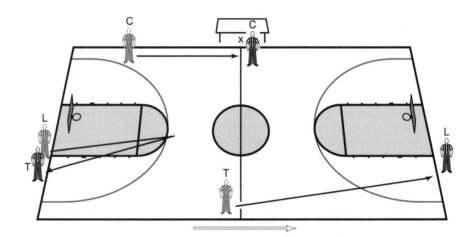

FIGURE 5.53   Lead official calling a foul in the backcourt going long.

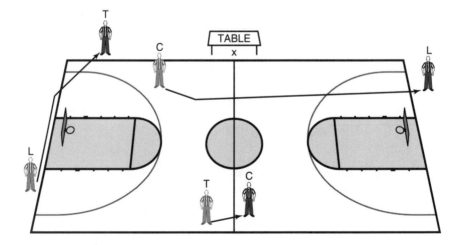

FIGURE 5.54   Center official calling a foul in the backcourt going long.

Figure 5.55 shows another situation when officials don't switch. The trail official calls and reports a foul in the frontcourt and the ball remains in the frontcourt with or without free throws. The trail official remains table side and resumes trail duties. The other two officials stay in their position.

FIGURE 5.55 Trail official calling a foul table side, staying in the frontcourt with or without free throws.

Free Throws

Free-throw duties in a three-person crew are similar to those in two-person crews, but there are some changes. In this section we'll look at general administrative duties; specific duties for the lead, center and trail officials; and the mechanics for when the defense gets the ball after a made free throw and after a technical, intentional or flagrant foul.

General Duties

The center and lead officials should make eye contact with each other and visually signal the number of throws. All officials should make sure that the lane spaces are properly occupied, and they should take a final look at the table before the free throw is administered. All officials are responsible for rebounding action and fouls that occur after the free thrower releases the ball. See figure 5.56 for the general responsibilities of each official.

After each foul but before the ball is put in play, officials should switch according to the diagrams in the previous section on fouls. The noncalling officials are responsible for initiating the switch after the foul has been reported.

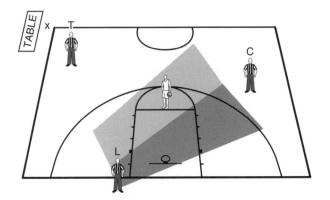

FIGURE 5.56   Lead, trail and center officials' areas of responsibility for free throws.

Lead Official

If you are lead official, secure the ball until the center and trail officials complete all signals and are in position. Once your crewmates are ready, step into the lane, visually and verbally indicate the number of throws (see figure 5.57), bounce the ball to the thrower, and back out of the lane, taking a position about four feet from the near lane line, approximately three feet off the end line table side.

FIGURE 5.57   Lead official indicating number of free throws.

Watch the first space on the near lane and all the lane spaces on the opposite side for violations and give the appropriate signal if either team violates (see figure 5.58 for a delayed defensive violation).

If the final throw is to be followed by a throw-in at the proper time, signal to start the clock.

FIGURE 5.58   Lead official signaling a defensive violation on a free throw.

Center Official

If you are the center official, assume your standard free-throw position, which is just behind the free-throw line extended, halfway between the near free-throw lane and the sideline. Observe the position of the thrower's feet in relation to the free-throw line and watch for a violation. Begin the visible count using a wrist flick.

Step toward the end line when the thrower releases the ball. Observe the flight of the ball, noting whether it goes through, contacts or misses the ring, and watch for goaltending or basket interference.

Signal to start the clock if the final throw or the first throw of a one-and-one is unsuccessful and the ball remains live.

Trail Official

If you are the trail official, take your position about 28 feet from the end line, near the side boundary opposite the center official. Observe players in the backcourt, and if conditions warrant, move into the backcourt. Be careful not to obstruct the view of the scorer, timer or team benches.

In addition to ensuring that the correct player attempts the throw and players are in the proper lane spaces, you should assist with free-throw violations and close down on the release, officiating the rebounding action.

Defense Gets the Ball

When the defensive team gets the ball after a free-throw attempt, follow these procedures.

Lead Official
If you are the lead official, you become the new trail official. After determining sideline responsibility, move along the sideline while covering backcourt play.

Center Official
If you are the center official, you remain as center official and after observing to evaluate any applied pressure, move downcourt to assume your normal position. When changing from one end of the court to the other, never turn your back on the players, but don't backpedal, either. Run downcourt while looking over your shoulder.

Trail Official
If you are the trail official, you become the new lead official. Move ahead of the ball along the sideline to the other end of the court (see figure 5.59). Be alert so you can get ahead of the ball on a fast break. Assist on three-point rulings on fast breaks if neither the center official nor the new trail official is in position to make the call.

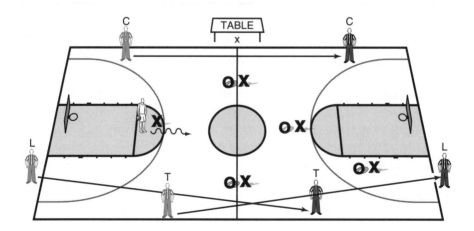

FIGURE 5.59   Transition when the defense gets the ball.

After a Technical, Intentional or Flagrant Foul

After a technical, intentional or flagrant foul, the official who calls the foul reports it and moves table side. If the technical foul is on a coach, the official opposite the table may want to switch with the calling official to help diffuse confrontation (see figure 5.60). The lead official should make sure the other officials are in position before putting the ball at the disposal of the free thrower.

FIGURE 5.60   Lead official going opposite the table after a technical foul call.

Following a free throw for a technical foul, the center official becomes the new trail official and administers the throw-in at the division line opposite the table (see figure 5.61). On an intentional or flagrant personal foul, the official responsible for the end line or sideline nearest the foul administers the throw-in.

FIGURE 5.61   Center official becoming the new trail official to administer the throw-in after a free throw for a technical foul.

Violations

The general mechanics for calling and reporting violations were covered in chapter 3 (see pages 45-47). In addition to those mechanics, you need to understand the procedures for closely guarded calls and for basket interference and goaltending violations.

When a dribbler is closely guarded, the lead, center and trail officials are responsible for the five-second closely guarded count (see figure 5.62, a-c) when it starts in their primary area. The responsible official should stay with the dribbler, even toward the other side and other official's area of responsibility, showing that you still have the initial count and that the offensive player is still closely guarded.

For basket interference and goaltending calls, the center and trail officials are responsible for the flight of the ball on a try. If the shot is taken in your primary area, your first responsibility is to stay with the shooter to make sure a foul has not occured. The outside off official (either the trail or the center) is responsible for watching the flight of the ball and, if necessary, moves to a position to more effectively cover areas of responsibility. The lead official should not watch the flight of the ball, focusing on rebounding fouls instead.

FIGURE 5.62   *(a-c)* Center official performing a visible count.

Time-Outs

The general mechanics for time-outs were covered in chapter 3 (see pages 48 through 49). Remember to have good posture and stay alert. During a 30-second time-out, the nonadministering officials stand at the top of the free-throw circle arc (see figure 5.63a). During a 60-second time-out, if you are the administering official take the ball to where it will be put in play (see figure 5.63b).

If play is to be resumed table side near the scorer or team benches, move out on the floor in line with the other two officials. Place the ball in front of, behind or on either side of your body to indicate the direction of play.

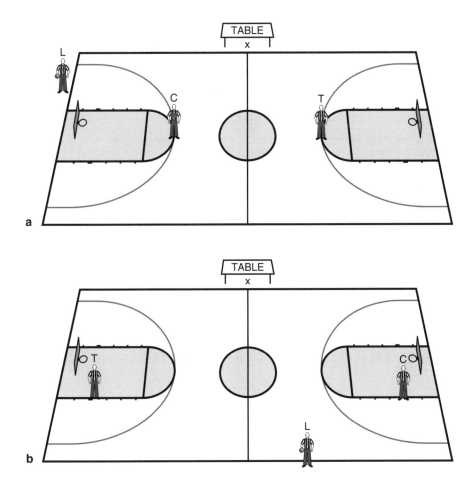

FIGURE 5.63 Lead, trail and center officials' positioning for a *(a)* 30-second time-out and *(b)* 60-second time-out.

If play is to be resumed with a free throw, the administering official should take a position on the free-throw line. The two other officials should be on the blocks (neutral zone), opposite and facing the scorer's table, as shown in figure 5.64, a and b.

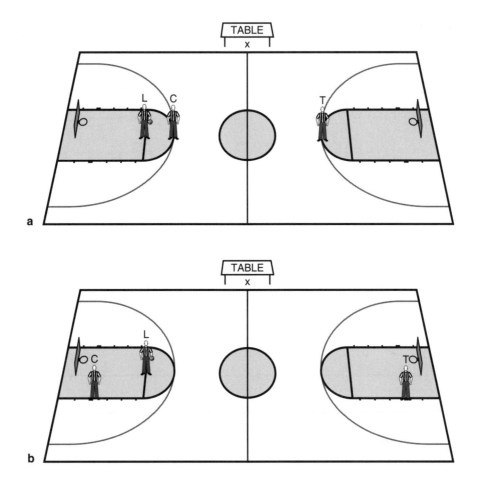

FIGURE 5.64   Lead, trail and center officials' positioning when play is resumed with a free throw after a *(a)* 30-second time-out and *(b)* a 60-second time-out.

Be ready to beckon properly reported substitutes into the game (see figure 5.65, a and b) and to give the scorer and timer any needed information. If activities on or off the court make it necessary, move to a safe location on or near the court during the time-out.

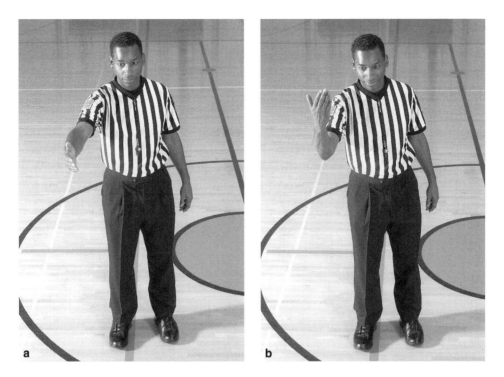

FIGURE 5.65   *(a and b)* Official beckoning a substitute into the game.

During the intermission between quarters the referee takes a position at the division line on the sideline opposite the table, indicating the direction of play with the placement of the ball (see figure 5.66). The umpires take a position on the blocks (neutral zone) opposite and facing each bench area.

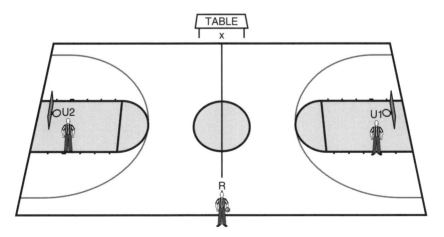

FIGURE 5.66   Referee and umpire positioning during intermission between quarters.

Don't visit with your crewmates unless you need to confer about a game situation. All officials are responsible for counting the players on each team as they enter the court. On a throw-in following an intermission, the administering official (referee) should sound a whistle before handing the ball to the thrower, indicating that play is about to begin.

Those are the mechanics for officiating in a crew of three. Remember to study chapter 3 in addition to this chapter when preparing to officiate in a three-person crew. Together these chapters provide the details you need to know to effectively operate with two other officials.

Now that you've completed the section on mechanics, it's time to test your knowledge of the rules and consider how you'd rule in various situations.

PART III

APPLYING THE RULES

CHAPTER 6

THE GAME

As you know from the *NFHS Basketball Rules Book,* there are 10 categories of rules:

- Rule 1: Court and Equipment
- Rule 2: Officials and Their Duties
- Rule 3: Players, Substitutions and Equipment
- Rule 4: Definitions
- Rule 5: Scoring and Timing Regulations
- Rule 6: Live Balls and Dead Balls
- Rule 7: Out of Bounds and Throw-Ins
- Rule 8: Free Throws
- Rule 9: Violations and Penalties
- Rule 10: Fouls and Penalties

In the next three chapters we'll consider cases under each of the 10 rules. For each rule we'll present several cases and then provide the appropriate rulings. These cases are meant to supplement close study of the *NFHS Basketball Rules Book* and help bring to life some of the situations you will face, but they by no means replace your need to thoroughly know the rules book. Use chapters 6 through 8 to test and augment your understanding of the rules.

In this chapter, we'll consider cases in the first four rules:

- Rule 1: Court and Equipment
- Rule 2: Officials and Their Duties
- Rule 3: Players, Substitutions and Equipment
- Rule 4: Definitions

Rule 1: Court and Equipment

Rule 1 covers the court and equipment: court lines, backboard padding, game balls, bench locations, and noise and sound restrictions. Here we'll present a few scenarios and their rulings. Consider how you'd respond in each situation and check your judgments against the answers beginning on page 126.

CASE 1: Game-Ball Dilemma

You're the referee for a game between Jamestown and Pittsfield. Before the game Pittsfield, the home team, presents a game ball that does not have the NFHS Authenticating Mark. Noting the problem, the Jamestown coach presents a ball that has the approved mark. Do you accept it as the game ball?

CASE 2: Changing the Location of a Team Bench

As York is warming up for its game at Brownsburg, the York coach complains to you, the referee, that the location of his or her team's bench means his or her players will have to go considerably farther than the home team to reach the reporting area. Should you make any changes to make the distance to report equal for both teams?

CASE 3: Sound Restrictions

Centralia is playing at Westwood in a game of high significance for both teams, who have a heated rivalry. The Westwood crowd is vociferous. Of the following three situations, which are legal?

1. The Westwood band plays during a live ball.
2. The electronic scoreboard plays broken-glass sound effects just after a missed Centralia field goal.
3. Westwood fans use artificial noisemakers during a Centralia player's free-throw attempt.

CASE 4: Not Hearing the Final Horn

Richmond leads Independence by one point in the final seconds of the fourth quarter in a game at Independence. An Independence player puts up a shot while in your coverage area. You don't hear the horn, which went off just before the shot, because of the crowd noise. The ball goes in and you signal a successful goal.

The referee definitely heard the horn before the Independence player released the shot, but you and the referee leave the playing area because the referee doesn't realize that you counted the goal. You aren't aware of the controversy until the scorer comes to your dressing room. At that point, you realize your mistake and know that the goal shouldn't have counted. Do you change your ruling, thus giving the win to Richmond?

Rule 2: Officials and Their Duties

Rule 2 pertains to the various duties of officials, including jurisdiction, unsporting behavior, disqualified players, correctable errors, accidental issues and more. Consider how you'd respond in the following situations and then check the answers beginning on page 127.

CASE 5: Going to the Bonus Too Early

Brownsburg is playing at Jamestown. A Jamestown player is fouled, and you erroneously award the player a one-and-one. The error is brought to your attention after the Jamestown player makes the first free throw. What do you do?

Consider how your ruling would be different if you discovered the error after the following:

1. The Jamestown player made both free throws.
2. The second free throw was missed and a Brownsburg player secured the rebound.
3. Both free throws were made and a Brownsburg player was in control of the ball, ready for the throw-in.
4. Both free throws were made and Brownsburg controlled the ball after a successful throw-in.

CASE 6: Questionable Three-Pointer

In a game at York, a Pittsfield player shoots from behind the three-point arc. You, the covering official, fail to give the signal for a successful three-pointer, and the scorer records the goal as two points. York quickly inbounds the ball and goes down for a score. Before Pittsfield inbounds the ball, the Pittsfield coach goes to the table and requests a 60-second time-out to discuss the error. What should happen?

Would your ruling be any different if the Pittsfield player made a shot from behind the arc, you signaled a successful three-pointer and the scorer recorded only two points?

Rule 3: Players, Substitutions and Equipment

This rule defines what is legal in terms of uniform numbers, number of players required, substitution situations, injuries and bleeding players, and more. Try your hand at the following situations and then check the answers beginning on page 128.

CASE 7: Illegal Numbers

A game between Westwood and Richmond is about to begin when the scorer discovers that two Richmond players are wearing numbers that are different than those listed in the score book. You are the referee, and the scorer brings the problem to your attention. What do you do?

Would your ruling be any different if two Richmond players were wearing the same number?

CASE 8: Substituting During a Time-Out

Centralia has called a 30-second time-out in a game against Independence. An Independence player reports to the scorer to enter the game as a substitute after the 20-second warning but before the time-out is over. Should you allow the substitution?

Would your ruling be different if the player reported before the 20-second warning signal? What if the substitute reported as the players were breaking the huddle and taking their positions on the floor just before the end of the time-out?

A substitution may be made during a time-out as long as the player reports before the warning horn.

CASE 9: Changing Shirts

In a game at York, a Jamestown player has to leave the game because blood had saturated the jersey. The Jamestown team packed no extra shirts with them. The Jamestown coach asks one of the substitutes to sacrifice a shirt so the player can return to the game. Is this legal?

Would your response change if York, understanding that Jamestown had no extra shirts, offered to give the Jamestown player a shirt that is not exactly the same color or style of Jamestown's shirts but would clearly identify the player as a Jamestown player?

Rule 4: Definitions

Rule 4 covers many situations, including airborne shooters, alternating possession, backcourt violations, illegal dribbling, intentional fouls and much more. See how you do with the following calls and then check the answers beginning on page 129.

CASE 10: Possible Backcourt Violation

Pittsfield is playing at Brownsburg. As Pittsfield is advancing the ball from its backcourt toward its frontcourt, a player passes to a teammate, who catches the ball while both feet are on the floor, one foot in the frontcourt, the other in the backcourt. The player who caught the pass lifts the foot in the backcourt and then puts it back on the floor, still in the backcourt. Is this a violation?

What if the foot in the frontcourt is lifted, pivoted on and then put in the backcourt?

CASE 11: Making the Call on an Intentional Foul

A Centralia player is driving in for a fast-break layup and is intentionally fouled while shooting. The ball goes in. What is your call?

What would your call be if the shooter was intentionally fouled in the following situations?

1. The two-point attempt does not go in.
2. The shooter is fouled in the act of shooting a successful three-point attempt.
3. The shooter is fouled in the act of shooting an unsuccessful three-point attempt.

CASE 12: Catching Your Own Shot

In a game against Independence, a Westwood player dribbles in close and attempts a shot near the baseline. The ball doesn't touch the backboard or the rim as it goes over the far side of the rim. The shooter recognizes the ball has been overshot and runs to the other side of the basket and catches the ball before it strikes the floor and no other player touches the ball. Is this a violation?

Would your response change if the shooter had caught an errant shot and then dribbled?

Answers

Here are the correct answers for each situation. Check them to see how you did.

Case 1: Game-Ball Dilemma

You shouldn't immediately accept the legal ball provided by the visiting team. Pittsfield may well have another ball that is legal, and you should exhaust that possibility before accepting the Jamestown ball. The rules book in no way prohibits using any legal ball for the game.

Case 2: Changing the Location of a Team Bench

You shouldn't make any changes to ensure that both teams travel the same distance to report. You have no authority to move the location of either bench, unless it involves player safety. Game management is responsible for bench location. Benches should be on the floor and the two team benches should be about the same distance from the table

Officials should ensure that balls provided by teams are legal and have the NFHS Authenticating Mark.

whenever possible. You should, however, report unusual bench locations to the state association office.

Case 3: Sound Restrictions

None of the three situations are legal. Here is how to respond in each situation:

1. Notify game management to instruct the Westwood band to play only during the permitted times, which do not include when the ball is live.
2. Instruct the scoreboard operator to stop the prohibited acts.
3. Have someone make a public-address announcement that the use of artificial noisemakers is prohibited at all times.

In all situations, if the problem persists it could result in a technical foul.

Case 4: Not Hearing the Final Horn

This is an unfortunate situation in which you learn too late that you were wrong. Once you and your crewmate have left the visual confines of the playing area, the final score is official and can't be changed. In situations like this, you must communicate with your crewmate and observe the activity of the official scorer before leaving the court so you can resolve any scoring or timing problems.

Case 5: Going to the Bonus Too Early

If you discover you have awarded the bonus too early and the Jamestown player has made the first free throw, you should cancel the successful free throw and give Jamestown the ball at the spot out of bounds nearest to where the foul occurred.

In the other situations, here are the correct rulings:

1. You discover the error after the Jamestown player makes both free throws. Cancel both free throws and give Jamestown the ball out of bounds at the correct spot.
2. You discover the error after the Jamestown player missed the second free throw and a Brownsburg player secured the rebound—see ruling number 4.
3. You discover the error after the Jamestown player made both free throws and a Brownsburg player was in control of the ball, ready for the throw-in—see ruling number 4.
4. You discover the error after the Jamestown player made both free throws and Brownsburg controlled the ball after a successful throw-in. Cancel the successful free throws and continue play with a throw-in by Brownsburg, because Brownsburg had the ball when the game was interrupted for the correction.

Case 6: Questionable Three-Pointer

This is a correctable error because it was detected before the second live ball after the error. The extra point is added to Pittsfield's total and the time-out is not charged to Pittsfield. The game continues with Pittsfield inbounding the ball. York's basket after the error counts.

Had you signaled for a three-pointer but the scorer gave only two points, the error could be corrected at any time until the final score is approved. So, in this case the same ruling applies: Add the extra point and resume play with Pittsfield inbounding the ball.

Case 7: Illegal Numbers

If either or both of the Richmond players' numbers have to be changed in the score book, you should assess Richmond one team technical foul. It doesn't matter how many numbers are changed; one technical covers all such situations. If, however, the Richmond coach does not request a change and neither player enters the game, there is no penalty.

If two Richmond players were wearing the same number, you would assess one team technical foul to Richmond. One player could retain the number, but the other would have to change to a number not already in use by the team.

Case 8: Substituting During a Time-Out

Because the Independence player reported after the 20-second warning, you should not allow entry, even if the player reported before the end of the time-out.

If, however, the player reported before the 20-second warning, entry would be permitted. If substitutes report as the players are breaking the huddle and returning to the court, they are not allowed to enter. Substitutions must be made before the warning signal.

Case 9: Changing Shirts

It is perfectly acceptable for the Jamestown player to wear a teammate's shirt. The scorer should note the change in the score book and the player can return to the game with the new uniform number. The substitute now wearing the bloody shirt cannot enter the game, however.

If York were to give Jamestown a jersey for the player to wear, and the shirt were not exactly the same color or style as that of the other Jamestown players, that would also be acceptable so long as it is clear to players, coaches and officials that the player in the borrowed jersey is a Jamestown player. Again, the scorer would note the new number and the player could return to the game.

Case 10: Possible Backcourt Violation

This is a backcourt violation. Once the Pittsfield player lifts the foot that is in the backcourt while the other foot is down in the frontcourt, the ball is in the frontcourt. Putting the foot back down again in the backcourt constitutes a violation.

If, however, the Pittsfield player lifts the frontcourt foot and then pivots and places it in the backcourt, there is no violation. As soon as the frontcourt foot is lifted, the player is in the backcourt, as a foot is still down in the backcourt. Placing the other foot in the backcourt doesn't change the position of the ball, which remains in the backcourt.

Case 11: Making the Call on an Intentional Foul

The basket counts and the Centralia player who was fouled receives two free throws for the intentional foul. After the free throws, Centralia gets the ball at the out-of-bounds spot nearest the foul.

If either the two-pointer or the three-pointer does not go in, the shooter gets the appropriate number of shots—two for the two-point attempt, three for the three-point attempt—and Centralia gets the ball at the out-of-bounds spot nearest the foul. If a three-point attempt goes in, the shot counts, the player gets two free throws and Centralia gets the ball at the out-of-bounds spot nearest the foul.

Case 12: Catching Your Own Shot

The Westwood shooter can catch an errant shot even though the ball does not touch the rim, the basket or another player; the player did not commit a traveling violation. It also wouldn't be a violation if the player dribbled the ball after catching the poor shot. The player could shoot again, dribble or pass. Team control ended when the ball was released on a try.

CHAPTER 7

PLAY

In chapter 6 you considered cases concerning the first four rules categories, including court and equipment, your duties as an official, and definitions of various aspects of the game. In this chapter we'll move on to these rules:

- Rule 5: Scoring and Timing Regulations
- Rule 6: Live Balls and Dead Balls
- Rule 7: Out of Bounds and Throw-Ins
- Rule 8: Free Throws

As with the last chapter, read each case and consider how you'd respond. Then check the answers beginning on page 134.

Rule 5: Scoring and Timing Regulations

This rule covers a lot of ground, including what is and isn't a try or tap for goal; three-point tries; three-tenths of a second or less on the clock; ending a quarter or extra period; time-out requests; timing mistakes and corrections; and more.

CASE 1: Counting the Shot

Richmond is playing at Jamestown. The game clock shows three-tenths of a second in the third quarter. A Richmond player is attempting a second free throw. The free-throw shot is missed, but a teammate taps the ball so that it leaves the hand before the horn sounds and goes in. Does the basket count?

What if the Richmond player had grabbed the missed shot, put up another shot—with the ball in flight before the horn sounded—and then went in?

CASE 2: Unruly Crowd

Late in a tense game between Independence and Pittsfield, you call a double foul on the two post players for pushing and shoving. It is the fifth

An error cannot be corrected once play has begun.

foul for both players. Some spectators shout derogatory comments, and some throw paper cups and other things onto the court. The entire crowd is in a hostile mood, though the negative comments and debris seem to be coming from the Pittsfield section. What should you do?

CASE 3: Overtime or Not

Centralia leads Brownsburg 62 to 60 in the fourth quarter when a Brownsburg player is fouled with no time left. The horn sounds immediately after the foul is called.

Brownsburg is not in the bonus, but your crewmate erroneously awards the Brownsburg player a one-and-one. The player makes both shots, tying the score.

Centralia controls the tap to begin overtime, and they score to take a 64 to 62 lead. Before the ball becomes live on the subsequent throw-in, the scorer alerts you of a potential correctable error. The game, says the scorer, shouldn't have gone into overtime, but should have ended with Centralia winning, 62 to 60. What do you do?

Rule 6: Live Balls and Dead Balls

This rule addresses when the ball is dead and when it's live, and how to rule in either case. Try your hand at the following situations and find out if you were correct by checking the answers beginning on page 135.

CASE 4: Simultaneous Fouls

A York player and a Westwood player begin fighting, and you stop play. A York substitute rushes onto the court but doesn't enter the fight. A Westwood substitute also comes onto the court and does participate in the fight. How do you rule, and how does play resume?

CASE 5: Double Violation on a Free Throw

A Richmond player is on the free-throw line and about to attempt a free throw when an Independence player, in a marked lane space, enters the lane prematurely. You properly signal the delayed violation and the Richmond player shoots the free throw. The shot doesn't go in and doesn't touch the rim. What's your ruling?

CASE 6: Foul During a Free Throw

Before the bonus, a Brownsburg player begins the free-throw motion. As the motion begins, a teammate fouls a Jamestown player with a push along the lane. What do you call?

Rule 7: Out of Bounds and Throw-Ins

This rule covers when a player is out of bounds and other out-of-bounds situations, throw-in spots, violations of the throw-in spot, the throw-in plane, and other issues surrounding out of bounds and throw-ins. Respond to the following cases and check the answers beginning on page 136 to see how you did.

CASE 7: Still Inbounds

In a game against York, a Pittsfield player blocks a pass near the end line. The ball falls to the court inbounds, but the Pittsfield player, off balance, steps off the court, returns inbounds, secures control of the ball and begins dribbling. Is this legal?

CASE 8: Location of the Throw-In

Richmond has just scored against Westwood, who is not in the bonus. A Westwood player is preparing for a throw-in, but before releasing the ball, a Richmond player fouls an inbounds Westwood player waiting near the end line for the throw-in. Where is the new throw-in spot? Where would it be if the following occurred?

1. A Richmond player fouled a Westwood player at the division line.
2. A Richmond player fouled a Westwood player beyond the division line.
3. There was no foul, but a Westwood player requested a time-out.

CASE 9: Leaving the Designated Throw-In Spot

An Independence player is out of bounds for a throw-in at a spot that you have designated. You have put the ball at the thrower's disposal. To avoid defensive pressure, the player takes several steps backward, but keeps one foot on or over the designated area before passing the ball inbounds to a teammate. Is this legal?

Rule 8: Free Throws

Rule 8 defines situations involving free throws, including placing the ball at the disposal of the shooter, lane space regulations, putting the ball into play and other issues. Answer the following questions and see how well you did by checking the answers in the next section on page 137.

CASE 10: Team Delay

A Jamestown player is fouled by a York player as a shot is attempted. You call the foul, report it and assume your position for the free throws. The York players are in position as well, and your crewmate, the administering official, has given all instructions and signals. However, three Jamestown players are huddling inside the lane. How should you handle this delay?

CASE 11: Lane Violation Plus a Technical

A Pittsfield player is at the free-throw line after having been fouled in the act of shooting. As the Pittsfield player puts up the first attempt, a player from Brownsburg steps into the lane, committing a lane violation. You signal the violation, and the shot misses.

The Brownsburg player then makes a comment that results in you charging a technical foul for unsporting conduct. Pittsfield requests a time-out, which you grant. How does play resume following the time-out?

CASE 12: Two Technical Fouls

A Centralia player has just made a shot against Richmond. During the dead-ball time immediately following this goal, a Richmond player is charged with a technical foul for using profanity toward the player who just scored. A few seconds later, a Centralia player taunts the Richmond player who was just charged with the technical, earning that player a technical foul.

What happens next? Should you award free throws, or are the fouls simultaneous?

Answers

In this section you'll find the correct rulings for the cases in this chapter. Check the answers to see how you did.

Case 1: Counting the Shot

The tapped shot counts. A tapped shot can count with three-tenths of a second or less on the clock if the ball leaves the player's hand before the horn sounds.

However, the grabbed rebound and resulting shot would not count, even if the ball were released before the horn sounds. Only a tap can score with three-tenths of a second or less on the clock.

Case 2: Unruly Crowd

You should ask the game or home management to control the spectators. If you can determine which team's spectators are involved you can charge a technical foul. However, you should use discretion in making such a call, because calling a foul on spectators typically doesn't defuse the situation and usually causes additional problems.

You should not forfeit the game due to spectator behavior. If game or home management can't restore order, you can suspend play. The game would then be continued later on from the point of interruption, unless the teams agree to end the game with the existing score or there are conference or state association rules that would direct you otherwise.

Case 3: Overtime or Not

The scorer is right: You can correct the error by taking two points away from Brownsburg. However, because the overtime period started, it cannot be canceled. So the score stands 64 to 60 in Centralia's favor (instead of 64 to 62), and the overtime continues with a Brownsburg throw-in.

Case 4: Simultaneous Fouls

The York and Westwood players who initiated the fighting are disqualified, as are the York and Westwood substitutes who came onto the floor. The York substitute doesn't have to enter into the fight to be disqualified; simply coming onto the floor earns a disqualification.

No free throws result from the double flagrant foul committed by the two players who began fighting or from the simultaneous technical fouls committed by the two substitutes. Charge each head coach with an indirect technical foul, and resume play with an alternating-possession throw-in from the division line opposite the table.

A substitute who comes onto the floor during a fight or likely fight will be disqualified even if the player does not participate in a fight.

Case 5: Double Violation on a Free Throw

This is a double violation. Unless another free throw follows, play should resume with an alternating-possession throw-in from a designated spot outside the end line.

Case 6: Foul During a Free Throw

If the foul occurs after the ball is in flight, the point counts if the ball goes in. If it doesn't go in, the shooter doesn't get a substitute free throw.

If the foul occurs before the ball is in flight, the ball becomes dead and the shooter is allowed an unhindered free throw.

The foul by the Brownsburg player during the free throw results in Jamestown being awarded the ball out of bounds at the spot nearest where the foul occurred, unless the free throw is successful. If the free throw is successful, Jamestown throws in from out of bounds anywhere along the end line.

Case 7: Still Inbounds

It's legal; the Pittsfield player is inbounds. The player didn't leave the court voluntarily, and didn't have control of the ball while out of bounds. After returning to the court and having inbounds status, it was legal to gain control of the ball.

Case 8: Location of the Throw-In

In the first situation, where the foul occurs near the end line, Westwood would throw in from anywhere out of bounds along the end line.

Here are the rulings for the other situations:

1. A Richmond player fouled a Westwood player at the division line. Westwood throws in from the spot out of bounds nearest to where the foul occurred.

2. A Richmond player fouled a Westwood player beyond the division line. Westwood throws in from the spot out of bounds nearest to where the foul occurred.

3. There was no foul, but a Westwood player requested a time-out. After the time-out Westwood throws in from anywhere out of bounds along the end line.

Case 9: Leaving the Designated Throw-In Spot

It's legal. The Independence player can move backward, forward or laterally within the designated area, so long as one foot stays on or over the designated area until the ball has been released. The player may also jump vertically and release the ball from the designated spot. Pivot-foot restrictions are not in place for a throw-in; the thrower must simply keep one foot on or over the spot until releasing the ball.

Case 10: Team Delay

Jamestown should be warned for delay. The scorer records this delay, and it is reported to Jamestown's head coach. Any subsequent delay for the same infraction by Jamestown during a free throw would result in a technical foul.

Case 11: Lane Violation Plus a Technical

The Pittsfield player who was at the line gets two free throws with the lane cleared. These are the shots for being fouled in the act of shooting. Pittsfield then gets two shots for the technical foul, which may be shot by any Pittsfield player or entering substitute. Following these shots, Pittsfield is awarded a throw-in at the division line across from the table.

Case 12: Two Technical Fouls

The fouls were close together, but they were not simultaneous. You should award free throws in the order that the fouls occurred: Centralia shoots two free throws first, and then Richmond shoots two free throws. The free throws can be attempted by any player of the offended team, including any eligible substitute. Following Richmond's free throws, Richmond gets a throw-in from the division line opposite the table.

CHAPTER 8

VIOLATIONS, FOULS AND PENALTIES

I n this chapter you'll consider situations concerning rules 9 and 10, which cover violations and fouls. These constitute the final two categories of rules in the *NFHS Basketball Rules Book*.

As with the previous two chapters, read the cases and decide how you'd respond. Then check the answers beginning on page 141.

Rule 9: Violations and Penalties

Rule 9 covers violations and their penalties. It details violations regarding play in the lane, throw-ins, boundary planes, dribbling, the 3-second and 10-second rules, closely-guarded situations and more.

CASE 1: Double Dribble
A Westwood player stops dribbling, jumps and releases a shot that is partially blocked by an Independence player. The shooter gains control of the blocked shot while still in the air, returns to the floor, dribbles to the basket and scores. Is this legal, or was there a double dribble?

CASE 2: Three-Second Violation
The Richmond post player is standing with one foot inside the three-second restricted area and the other outside the area, positioned to receive a pass. To avoid being called for a three-second violation, the player lifts the foot that's in the lane, and, without touching it to the floor outside the lane, plants it again in the lane. Three seconds elapse, including the time that the foot was lifted and neither foot was touching in the lane. Is this a violation?

CASE 3: 10-Second Violation
In a game against Independence, a Pittsfield player is in the team's backcourt and has dribbled for nine seconds. The player then throws a chest pass to a teammate in the frontcourt. The ball is in the air when you reach your 10-second count. Is this a violation?

Would your response be different if the Pittsfield player made a bounce pass to the frontcourt and the ball struck in the frontcourt, but no one touched it before the 10 seconds expire?

CASE 4: Closely Guarded Violation

A Brownsburg player dribbles across the division line, closely guarded by a Centralia player. While in the team's frontcourt, the Brownsburg player dribbles for three seconds and then holds the ball for four seconds before passing the ball to a teammate. Should you have called a closely guarded violation after five seconds had passed (three seconds of dribbling and the first two seconds of holding the ball)?

Rule 10: Fouls and Penalties

This rule defines fouls and the penalties that come with them. Among the areas covered are team technicals, unsporting acts, delaying return following a time-out, dunking and grasping, contacting the backboard and

much more. Be sure to study your rules book to be well-versed in all the situations that rule 10 encompasses.

Check your knowledge of rule 10 by responding to the following questions and then checking the answers beginning on page 142.

CASE 5: Reporting Infraction

York is playing in a game at Westwood. A York substitute reports to the scorer and then enters the court without being beckoned. What should you do in this situation?

Would your response be different if the substitute had gone directly from the team bench to the court without reporting in or being beckoned?

If a foul occurs while a shot is in the air, it will be penalized.

CASE 6: Double Violation

As a shot by a teammate is on its way to the basket, a York player charges into a Brownsburg opponent. Another Brownsburg player then commits basket interference. Both teams are in the bonus. How do you rule?

Would your ruling be any different if a York player had committed basket interference?

CASE 7: Post Defense

In a game between Centralia and Westwood, the Centralia post player is being fronted by a defender. The Centralia guard, who has the ball near the top of the key, makes a high pass over the head of the Westwood defender. The Centralia post player moves toward the basket to catch the pass.

As the pass is made, another Westwood defender moves into the path of the Centralia post player and assumes a guarding position before the Centralia player catches the pass. The Westwood defender has the feet set, the Centralia player does not leave the ground and crashes into the defender as the pass is csught. Who is the foul on?

Answers

See how well you know rules 9 and 10 by checking the answers to this chapter's questions.

Case 1: Double Dribble

This move is legal. The player's control of the ball, as well as team control, ended when the ball was released on the shot attempt. When the blocked shot was recovered, the player was free to dribble, just as if a pass was cought or a rebound secured.

Case 2: Three-Second Violation

This is a three-second violation. The three-second count is not terminated when the Richmond player lifts a foot from the lane. Had the player placed that foot outside the lane so that both feet were outside the lane, the count would have ended. But in this case your count should continue.

Remember that there is no three-second count during rebounding action or a throw-in. The count for a player in the restricted area ends when a try for goal begins.

Case 3: 10-Second Violation

It is a 10-second violation, because the ball has not gained frontcourt status. You should award Independence the ball at the out-of-bounds spot closest to where the Pittsfield player released the ball in the backcourt.

If a ball is still in the backcourt at the 10-second count, a 10-second violation will be called.

Had the Pittsfield player made a bounce pass that bounced in the frontcourt even though no player touched it, and it touched in the frontcourt before 10 seconds expired, it would be legal. The ball gains frontcourt status as soon as it touches the floor in the frontcourt.

Case 4: Closely Guarded Violation
No closely guarded violation occurred. Had the Brownsburg player dribbled for five seconds while being closely guarded the whole time, a violation would have occurred. A new five-second count began when the player picked up the dribble and looked to pass.

Case 5: Reporting Infraction
You should call a technical foul on the York substitute for entering the game without being beckoned. It doesn't matter if the player reported in; players must be beckoned before entering the court.

Likewise, you would assess a technical against the York substitute for entering the court having neither reported nor been beckoned. You would assess one technical in this case even though the player committed two infractions.

Case 6: Double Violation
You should penalize the foul by the York player and the basket interference by the Brownsburg player. York gets two points or three points, depending on whether the attempt was for a two-pointer or three-pointer. The Brownsburg player who was fouled then gets a one-and-one. Had the bonus not been in effect, Brownsburg would have received the ball out of bounds at the spot closest the foul. If the ball were awarded on the baseline, the player inbounding the ball from Brownsburg would be able to run the end line.

If the basket interference were committed by York, the ball would be dead and no points awarded even if the ball went in, and the Brownsburg player who was fouled in the bonus situation would get a one-and-one.

Case 7: Post Defense

The foul is on the Westwood defender, because guarding position was established before the Centralia player had control of the ball and therefore the defense must give the player a stride or two to be legal.

   If the Westwood player had come over to defend the Centralia player after the pass was caught, was on the ground and had control of the ball, then no distance or time limit would be involved.

NFHS Officiating Basketball Signals

Start clock

Stop clock

Stop clock for jump/held ball

Stop clock for foul

Stop clock (bird dog)

Beckon substitutes

60-second time-out

30-second time-out

Fouls

Technical foul

Blocking

Holding

Hand check

Pushing or charging

Illegal use of hands

Player-control foul

Intentional foul

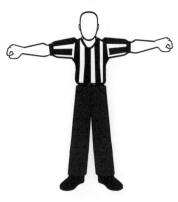

Double foul

Violations

Traveling

Illegal dribble

Three-second violation

Over-and-back or
palming or carrying
the ball

Five- or ten-second
violation
(use both hands for ten)

Free throw,
designated spot
or other violation

Excessively swinging
arm(s)/elbow(s)

Kicking

Information

Visible count

Directional signal

Throw-in, free throw or designated spot

No score

Goal counts

Points scored

Number of free throws

Delayed lane violation

Three-point field goal attempt

Successful three-point field goal

GLOSSARY

airborne shooter—a shooter who releases the ball while in the air; the shooter is airborne until returning to the floor.

alternating possession arrow—an arrow at the officials' table that indicates which team gets the ball on a jump ball, the beginning of a quarter other than the first quarter and so on.

backcourt violation—a player of the team in control of the ball cannot be the first to touch the ball after it has been in the frontcourt, if the player or a teammate last touched it or was touched by the ball in the frontcourt before it went into the backcourt.

basket interference—occurs when a player touches the ball or any part of the basket while the ball is on or within the basket or the imaginary cylinder above the basket.

blocking—illegal personal contact that impedes the progress of an opponent with or without the ball.

bonus free throw—the second free throw awarded for a common foul, except a player-control foul, beginning with a team's seventh foul in each half.

charging—illegal personal contact caused by pushing or moving into an opponent's torso.

closely guarded—occurs when a player is in control of the ball in the frontcourt and is legally guarded by an opponent who is within six feet while the player is holding or dribbling the ball.

continuous motion—applies to a try or tap for field goal, starting with the try or with the touching on a tap, and ending when the ball is clearly in flight.

control, player and team—a player is in control while holding or dribbling a live ball inbounds. A team is in control when one of its players is in control, while a live ball is being passed among teammates and during an interrupted dribble.

correctable error—an error that, by the rules, an official can correct. Most correctable errors pertain to free throws. All correctable errors involve a score.

double dribble—a violation occurring when a player dribbles again after stopping the first dribble. It is not a double dribble if the player loses control of the ball because it was batted by a defender or because the ball is fumbled and it is then touched by another player.

foul—an infraction of the rules that is charged and penalized.

free throw—the opportunity given a player to score a point by an unhindered shot from within the free-throw semicircle.

goaltending—occurs when a player touches the ball during a field-goal or free-throw attempt while the ball is in its downward flight, above the basket, has a chance of going in and is not touching an imaginary cylinder that has the basket ring as its lower base.

held ball—occurs when opponents have their hands so firmly on the ball that control can't be obtained by either one without undue roughness. Also occurs when an opponent places a hand or hands on the ball and prevents an airborne player from throwing or shooting.

holding—illegal personal contact with an opponent that interferes with freedom of movement.

incidental contact—contact with an opponent that is permitted.

kicking the ball—intentionally striking the ball with any part of a leg.

pivot—takes place when a player holding the ball steps once, or more than once, in any direction with the same foot while the other foot, called the pivot foot, is kept at its point of contact with the floor.

screen—a legal action by a player who, without causing contact, delays or prevents an opponent from reaching a desired position.

shooting—the act of shooting begins with the start of the try or tap and ends when the ball is clearly in flight, and includes the airborne shooter.

technical foul—a player or a team can be assessed a technical foul for a number of illegal acts.

10-second violation—when a team is in continuous control of a ball that is in their backcourt for 10 seconds.

three-second violation—when a player remains for three seconds in the free-throw lane between the end line and the farther edge of the free-throw line while the ball is in team control in the frontcourt.

throw-in—a method of putting the ball in play from out of bounds.

traveling—moving a foot or feet in excess of the prescribed limits while holding the ball.

verticality—from a legal guarding position, a defender can rise or jump vertically and occupy the space within a vertical plane. The player's hands and arms can be extended within this plane.

Note: The italicized *f* following page numbers refers to figures.

ABOUT THE AUTHOR

Officiating Basketball was written by the American Sport Education Program (ASEP) in cooperation with the National Federation of State High School Associations (NFHS). Based in Indianapolis, the NFHS is the rules authority for high school sports in the United States. Hundreds of thousands of officials nationwide and throughout the world rely on the NFHS for officiating guidance. ASEP is a division of Human Kinetics, based in Champaign, Illinois, and has been a world leader in providing educational courses and resources to professional and volunteer coaches, officials, parents and sport administrators for more than 20 years. ASEP and the NFHS have teamed up to offer courses for high school officials through the NFHS Officials Education Program.

NFHS Officials Education Program

ONLINE EDUCATION FOR ON-THE-GO OFFICIALS

NFHS OFFICIATING PRINCIPLES COURSE

An NFHS Officials Education Program Course

BEGIN

developed by the American Sport Education Program
A Division of Human Kinetics

OFFICIALS EDUCATION PROGRAM

American Sport Education Program
A DIVISION OF HUMAN KINETICS

© 2004 by Human Kinetics Publishers, Inc.

Late-night games.
Weekend tournaments.
Pregame preparation.
Postgame reflection.

As an official, just because you keep track of time doesn't mean you have any. So instead of taking even more time out to attend another officials clinic, explore the timesaving, schedule-friendly online courses offered through the **NFHS Officials Education Program.**

A joint effort between the **National Federation of State High School Associations (NFHS)** and the **American Sport Education Program (ASEP),** the NFHS Officials Education Program features a two-part, Internet-delivered curriculum covering officiating principles and sport-specific methods based on NFHS rules.

Available now is ***NFHS Officiating Principles,*** a course applicable to all officials regardless of their sport. The course shows you how to determine your officiating philosophy and style, improve communication, develop decision-making skills, manage conflict, understand legal responsibilities, manage your officiating career, and much more.

Coming soon: ***Officiating [Sport] Methods*** courses for softball, football, soccer, basketball, wrestling, and baseball cover the sport-specific methods and mechanics of officiating as they apply to NFHS rules and regulations. The officiating [sport] book that you have in your hands serves as the text for the course. Check the ASEP Web site at www.ASEP.com for updates on course availability.

NFHS Officials Education Program offers you the continuing education you need as an official on a schedule that's right for you. Registration fees are only $75 per course and include a course text, CD-ROM, study guide, exam, and entry into the National Officials Registry. For more information, or to register for a course, visit **www.ASEP.com** or call ASEP at **800-747-5698.**

OFFICIALS EDUCATION PROGRAM

NFHS

American Sport Education Program
A DIVISION OF HUMAN KINETICS